POLICE DOGS

and

their training

by

Reginald Arundel

EX-SUPERINTENDENT
YORKSHIRE WEST RIDING CONSTABULARY

PRICE **3**/- net

Picking up the Scent

POLICE DOGS
AND
THEIR TRAINING

1.—THE POLICE DOG'S HISTORY.

Police dogs were used to assist in bringing to justice the breaker of laws when the word Police was almost unknown. The first Police dog was the bloodhound, a breed of great antiquity and of majestic appearance and demeanour, remarkable for his large pendant ears, bloodshot haw, and sonorous note. This hound, held in high esteem amongst our ancestors, was used to recover any game that had escaped from the hunter, or had been killed and stolen out of the forest. But it was still more employed in hunting thieves and robbers by their footsteps.

Coming to more recent times, but still before the establishment of Police Forces, bloodhounds were used in certain districts lying between England and Scotland which were infested with robbers and marauders; a tax was laid on the inhabitants for maintaining them, and there was a law in Scotland that whoever denied entrance to one of these dogs should be treated as an accessory to the crime. In the latter part of the 18th century several associations for the prosecution of felons procured and trained bloodhounds principally for the detection of sheep stealers. To-day this hound is in use by various Police Forces, for tracking criminals and missing persons, and several striking instances of success are on record.

In one capacity the bloodhound can boast superior skill over all other breeds, *i.e.*, picking out a line of scent, and here I may remark· in making a selection from these hounds always choose the one with the most wrinkle about the skull and cheeks, and loose skin on the neck. Apart from his powers of scent the bloodhound possesses few qualities to recommend him as a Police dog, though owing to the almost supernatural abilities a credulous public ascribe to him, he acts as a useful deterrent to crime in the neighbourhood where he is kept. His worst fault is his ineradicable timidity; an express thundering over a bridge, or a man threatening with a stick, are often sufficient to turn him from the trail. If given corporal punishment or even harshly-spoken to, he will frequently sulk and refuse to work, and there is no other breed that is shy and nervous to such an extreme degree. Somerville (1692–1742), dealing with this hound writes:

> Unerring he pursues till at the cot
> Arrived, and seizing by his guilty throat
> The caitiff vile, redeems the captive prey,
> So exquisitely delicate his sense.

Whilst being quite prepared to admit the unerring pursuit and delicate sense, whatever bloodhounds were capable of in Somerville's time, it would be difficult to find a present-day bloodhound which would seize anyone, or could even be relied upon to defend his master when attacked. In spite of these defects, however, the Royal Irish Constabulary found him useful in their struggle with Sinn Fein. Taken to the scene of an ambush his marvellous scent on more than one occasion was the means of causing the arrest of participators in the affair who had taken refuge in the hills miles away.

After the " Peeler " came into being the " canine detective " suffered eclipse for a time, and it is on the Continent we first hear of him again. Fiction has made us familiar with the French Police dog, but it was in Germany that the subject was studied in the most thorough manner.

In 1896 experiments were made with various breeds and ultimately the **German Sheep Dog** (known in this country as the **Alsatian Wolf Dog**) was selected as possessing the most intelligence necessary for the purpose; a process of selective breeding and intensive training was undertaken, and now every Police division in Germany has its kennel of these trained dogs.

The breed was introduced into this country after the War, and in some quarters is a great favourite for Police work. Here a word of warning may be useful. The vogue of this breed in England led to the importation of low-grade dogs, the name alone being sufficient for many buyers. The name " Alsatian " is no guarantee of high intelligence, any more than is " Airedale," and both may be dull-witted and of no value as either Police or Watch-dogs.

The **Great Dane** is another breed originally imported from Germany, and though not always to be depended upon when other dogs are near, is without doubt a capital bodyguard, though hardly adaptable for general Police work.

The **Airedale** in many quarters has proved of great value for all-round Police work. He was used in the L.N.E.R. Docks at Hull, Hartlepool and Middlesbrough, and after his advent there was a marked decrease in thefts, fires and wilful damage. These canine dock detectives undergo a thorough training, and may be said to rank among the most efficient Police dogs in the world. This breed has also proved its worth in the suburbs of Liverpool, and to many a rural Constable he is an invaluable assistant, and on the Continent, where he is also used for Police duties, can hold his own with any of the native varieties. Colonel Richardson, Commandant of the War Dogs' School, where dogs of all breeds were trained during the first world war, has expressed the opinion that as a bodyguard the British Airedale was the master of them all.

The **Mastiff.** One of the oldest British breeds, kept to guard person and property ever since the Romans landed in Britain. The popular impression that the Mastiff when loosed from his kennel is a dangerous brute, is a wrong one. A well-trained Mastiff—his training calls for considerable tact—may be taken anywhere, and he is more trusty than any of the larger breeds. For Police work in general the Old English Mastiff is not so suitable as the **Bull-Mastiff.** This breed since it was first evolved has been a great favourite with gamekeepers as a protection against poachers. It is only of recent years that the Police have taken him up, and it was not until 1925 that the National Bull-Mastiff Police Dog Club was founded with the idea of specially training him for Police work. Faithful, fearless but not ferocious, with a good nose for tracking, he should be a success. Indeed, those Constables who have already adopted him, say they want no other dog and are unanimous in their opinion that for Police work he is quite on a par with the Alsatian or the Airedale.

The **Retriever** has been described by an expert as prepared to take on any class of work required of him as a "general utility dog." He makes a good guard, and trained for water-work is a very suitable breed for Constables whose beats are in close proximity to waterways. He has also good scenting powers and is endowed with both pluck and sagacity.

The **Kerry Blue Terrier.** This blue-grey, shaggy-headed breed, is another that has been found adaptable for Police work, as he is usually full of intelligence and vitality. It has been said, and with truth, that he makes the greatest fighting machine in the world when the necessity arises.

These do not exhaust the list: there are others one might mention, one, perhaps, in particular, the **Dobermann Pinscher,** spoken of as the dog with the human brain. But whatever breed is one's fancy, it should ever be borne in mind that the individual dog is of much more importance than the breed. Specimens of all breeds are to be met with, loose, flabby, slack-loined lymphatic animals, delicate feeders without energy or spirit, which are a waste of time to attempt to train. Also, it should be remembered, that for reasons given in the following section, whilst a thoroughbred is the best selection, pedigree and performance are two very different things.

2.—CHOOSING A DOG.

The best selection is undoubtedly a thoroughbred. There is a very prevalent theory that mongrels are more intelligent then thoroughbreds, and though some particular mongrels may be intelligent, they are only the exceptions that prove the rule that a crossbred at best is never to be depended upon; and for one good dog thus obtained there will be found on an average twenty very indifferent or bad dogs; in fact, you generally find united the worst qualities of the two without any of the good qualities, for which the two breeds are most highly prized. Select a middle-sized breed. The larger breeds are too heavy, too slow, too dangerous, and their upkeep is expensive. The smaller breeds are too weak and their insignificant appearance makes little or no impression on the malefactor. Choose a young dog and preferably a bitch, as they are more affectionate, easier to teach, less trouble in the lead, and often with a finer nose. It should not be more than nine weeks old and of parents that were sharp and courageous. Choose also one of the smooth-haired breed, as long-coated dogs are hampered in their duties in wet or damp weather, etc. The head should be large, as dogs with small heads seldom show superior intelligence or smartness. The teeth should be intact and unblemished; in fact, of snow-white colour in young dogs. The lower jaw must never project or stand far behind the upper one or extend too much behind the ears. The fangs should be short, which gives more power. The colour of the nose is indifferent, but it should always be moist and cool. The eyes should be clear; matter, slime or scurf are signs of disease. For Police work a dog with a medium-sized neck will be found to answer best. The paws should be short and well closed, and the front feet vertical. The chest should be broad and large, and the hind legs strong, with long muscles.

As it is of the utmost importance to be able to judge whether a young dog will be likely to turn out useful for Police purposes, there are three things it is first of all necessary to know. Whether the dog has

1.   A perfect eyesight.

2.   A perfect ear.

3.   A perfect nose.

And it is only by the closest observation that these three qualities can be detected, but the livelier the dog is the better the chance of success.

A Police dog must be sharp and courageous. Accordingly it is advisable to watch if the young dog exhibits signs of these qualities. For instance, if he

(a)   Attacks cats.

(b)   Barks madly at them.

(c)   Attacks other dogs.

(d)   Barks at strangers.

(e)   Goes for the legs of tramps.

(f)   Wags his tail when feeding and will not allow other dogs or animals to approach; raises his hair and growls when disturbed. All these are signs that the puppy will turn out a courageous dog. A puppy that feeds with his tail between his legs is sure to turn out soft and nervous, and utterly worthless for Police purposes.

3.—GENERAL ADVICE TO TRAINERS.

It has been said there is a something intangible which differentiates the great from the average detective and that what it is no one knows, not even those who have it. This remark is applicable to the dog trainer. Apart from those whom one may broadly classify as good, bad or indifferent, now and again the trainer is met who with his dog-magic and instinctive handling seems to have been born for this work. One recognizes that he has a wonderful and mysterious power over dogs, a gift he appears able to exercise no one knows how, and least of all himself. All dogs that go through his hands obey him instinctively as it were and never forget him. Almost without word or signal, he influences and directs them. Needless to say, a trainer such as this is rare, otherwise the following advice would be superfluous.

It is necessary for the trainer to have a good general knowledge of the nature, likes and dislikes of the particular dog he intends to train, as well as a satisfactory acquaintance with the properties and peculiarities of the whole breed. Above all, patience with the young dog is absolutely essential. As the mother and the teacher plod along patiently with the education of the child, so, and more so, is patience needed in a young dog's trainer. As there are times when a human being is both physically and mentally unfit for work, so it happens that occasionally the dog is unable to accomplish his task. Only from a dog which has completed his first year can be expected really good and intelligent work. The training must be done with kindness; by that alone can one make a true, faithful and self-sacrificing companion. With the whip or stick one only succeeds in producing a slave. The Police whistle should be the only kind used, so that the dog can distinguish it from the ordinary ones used in the street.

To use a whistle well requires patience, temper and experience. It should be done not loudly, but low, and not too much of it, or it may happen that the dog will become weary of it and you, and will pay no attention. Use it sparingly, but take care it is always obeyed and followed.

In such a way and manner should the young dog be trained that he feels it a punishment to be spoken to harshly or not at all, and he must be daily taught that he must not do what he likes, but what he is expected to do. If cruelty of any description has any part in the training of a Police dog, failure in the dog's work will be the inevitable result.

Trainers must realize that every dog at birth is endowed with a definite mental capacity, which will be found to vary very much, some dogs appearing to exhibit instinct merely, others evincing a degree of acuteness very similar to reason. This mental capacity does not increase or improve after maturity. Therefore as is pointed out in Article 3 in the following section, training merely serves to bring out such intelligence as the dog receives at birth and is not in any way the result of training as some seem to imagine. A dog of poor natural endowment cannot be trained for Police duties.

The bringing out of the dog's intelligence is done by repeating the lessons laid down—dogs, like humans, learn by repetition—simple ones to begin with, and as they are mastered those of more difficulty, always assuming the dog shows enough aptitude and ability to undertake the advanced course. Trainers will note the insistence on praise and the giving of the " tit-bit " for good work. These are incentives to greater efforts for—again like humans—the stronger the incentive the greater the pupil's diligence. A reward when the dog does right, gentle correction when he does wrong.

In this connection the animal's temper is an object that the trainer must not lose sight of; some dogs require frequent correction, while with others the mildest treatment and encouragement are indispensable. Trainers will observe that corporal punishment should never be given to a dog unless under absolute control; in fact, the dog should not be suffered to move till by a word or two of caution, spoken in a mild tone, his alarm is dissipated and trainer and dog are reconciled. Foolish, passionate men may be observed to let their dogs run away immediately the punishment is over, and to aim another blow at them as they are going away; nothing can be more censurable than this, for when the dog next commits a fault, and you wish to chastise him he will not allow you to approach sufficiently near to lay hold of him. The safest method of punishment is that laid down in Exercise 16 and is always effective when, as frequently happens, the young dog manifests an inclination to hunt sheep. A dog should be corrected, in fact, the moment he is observed to display the slightest inclination even to notice sheep, as he will, if not checked, first look and set, then chase, and ultimately worry them. When once dogs have tasted mutton they are never to be trusted and cannot be cured by this or any other mode short of confinement or death.

In regard to poultry, the evil is not so great, nor the disposition to worry so difficult to subdue, and there are better, as well as more frequent, opportunities of observation.

During the training exercises apart from the words of command the less the dog is spoken or whistled to the better. During the training the dog should never be suffered to go out but in company with the trainer.

He is thus accustomed to obey one person only, and becomes perfectly familiar with his mode and manner.· If dogs become subject to many masters they cannot be expected to be perfect.

The trainer should give his words of command in as low a voice as possible and avoid any unnecessary calls or whistling. He must not drag at the line, nor yet chide or punish the dog, but coax him and praise him in a low voice so as to keep him working.

The trainer should always take care that before beginning work the dog's bowels have been thoroughly moved and that he has quenched his thirst. Let him have his accustomed food regularly, but when he has any heavy work in front of him a good meal of flesh meat is advisable a few hours before starting. As to his bodily temperature, that can be judged from the coldness of his nose. The bodily welfare of his dog should always be the trainer's first care, and he should not be made to work at any time that he is obviously unwell.

In conclusion, the trainer should ever bear in mind the fact that the best Police dog can in a very few days be spoilt and made absolutely worthless by improper handling.

As I have already said, for it will bear repetition, train with kindness. Far better let a fault go by now and then than meet every peccadillo red-handed. You can always give a whipping—you cannot undo it. As often as not—especially when it is a matter of scent—the dog is right, the man is wrong, and more dogs are ruined with the whip than without it. Don't use anything heavier than a light switch; don't give a lot of blows, but one—not that if you can help it.

See the lessons are not prolonged; stick to the time-table. The young dog is soon tired, and this leads to boredom, and boredom spells careless work.

4.—THE TRAINING OF THE POLICE DOG.

1. Early, good and sound training brings out the good and extirpates the bad qualities in a boy and makes him turn out a gentleman. So in like manner will be brought out the capabilities of a dog specially adapted to assist, protect and serve his master.

2. As running, jumping, etc., are necessary to develop the child's body, and thus indirectly his mind, likewise the young dog requires plenty of exercise, and without it only develops into a lazy, clumsy brute, without passions or intelligence.

3. Training a dog means nothing else but to minimise or eradicate inborn bad or useless proclivities, and to bring out and perfect his good and useful qualities and propensities.

4. Experience shows that bad management of young dogs spoils their future usefulness for proper training. Hence great care is needed not to make them shy or frightened animals before ever they are fit and old enough to be trained.

5. To be able to train a dog successfully his individual qualities and propensities have to be carefully observed and studied.

6. Up to six months of age no dog is responsible for his actions; he is too stupid to know the why and the wherefore, consequently must not be punished, otherwise he runs the danger of being useless for successful training.

7. Only the trainer should feed and play with the dog, and during the time of training he must be well fed and cared for. If children or other persons handle or play with the dog, he is sure to get muddle-headed, playful, superficial, erratic, untrustworthy, headstrong, and often snappish or vicious. The young dog only has the sense of self-preservation; he likes, clings to and follows him that feeds and caresses him; later on this liking and clinging develop into love, gratitude and faithfulness.

8. As soon as the trainer has finished playing with the young dog he must replace him in the kennel. Should the dog start yowling, a shot or two from a catapult, saying " Quiet," will soon teach him to stop it at the word of " Quiet," and after a short time altogether. Dogs that have not been taught in this way are sure later on to join other dogs when yowling or barking.

9. Shortly before feeding time, say a quarter of an hour, but never longer than half an hour, the trainer should take the four months' old puppy into his room, or house, and watch him closely whilst playing with him. If the dog gives any signs of going to mess, return him quickly into his kennel. In case he has messed, take him gently, saying " Shame," and put him back. The man who pushes the dog's nose into the excrement has no idea of training dogs, and lays the foundation for future bad faults of character. A trained dog can be made house-clean in a moment by using a slight punishment.

5.—FOLLOWING THE SCENT.

(*Exercises* 53 *to* 63.)

Scent is an effluvium which is constantly issuing from the pores of all animal substances, and consists of minute particles which, driven by the wind, come in contact with the olfactory nerves of the dog and enable him to discover the proximity of the object of pursuit. It also clings to the ground whereon one walks, also to one's personal belongings, or to any object one handles.

The scent of each human being or animal is different, as is evident from the fact that any common cur will hunt out his master or his master's horse distinctly from all others.

This scent frequently alters in the same day; it may be said to depend chiefly on two things—the condition of the ground and the temperature of the air, which should be moist without being wet; when both are in this state the scent is then perfect, and *vice-versa*, when the ground is hard and dry there seldom will be much scent. It lies badly with a north or an east wind; a southerly wind without rain and a westerly one that is not rough are the best. Storms in the air seldom fail to destroy scent. Fog, as a rule, is bad for it, as is also frost; and when frost is going off scent never lies. It lies best in the richest soils, and is most difficult to pick up along much frequented roads. To expect a dog to follow a specific scent on the pavement of crowded city streets is to betray a lamentable ignorance of the subject. Experiments were made in London with bloodhounds at the time of the Jack the Ripper murders but, of course, without any success.

Failure in following up scent is sometimes owing to the dog's olfactory organs being affected. This will frequently be found to arise from colds, costiveness or other causes, which a dose or two of opening physic seldom

Two Mastiff Police Dogs

An Alsatian Police Dog

fails to remove. A little sulphur or syrup of buckthorn will generally have the desired effect.

Some dogs possess much better noses than others, but as a rule all dogs with broad heads have superior organs of smell, and the size of the ears is in some degree another criterion of this sense of smell.

Like most other faculties, this sense of smell is improved by practice, and it will be a long time before perfection is attained in the ten exercises laid down, and each one should be mastered thoroughly before the next is attempted. During training the dog should not be allowed to follow any scent except on the line and according to orthodox methods, otherwise the dog in his excitement and eagerness is liable to form the habit of opening out on fresh tracks, either human or, what is more likely, game, if there is any about.

Dogs which are kept in the country will always be found to have a superior sense of smell to those quartered in towns.

Difficulty in opening up the trail is, in many instances, due to unsuitable weather conditions supervening since the criminal left the scene of his crime, or, on the other hand, the scent of his footprints may have been too much weakened and mixed by the footprints of others. There are all kinds of circumstances and accidents which may happen in this class of work, so as to make success very difficult, and where the dog has been properly trained and is in a healthy condition, you may be sure that the failure is not due to any fault of his.

In view of the way in which atmospheric conditions affect scent, when requested to take up an actual case enquiries should always be made as to whether there has been any strong wind, rain, snow or frost since the matter occurred, and the period of time that has elapsed; also if it is definitely known that there is a specific scent to be picked up, unmixed with that of others. All these are points to take into consideration, first in coming to a decision as to whether the attempt is practicable, and, secondly, in the working of the trail.

Experience tells us that difference of soil alters the scent, and it has been observed that in some particular spots, be the temperature of the air what it may, dogs can never carry a scent across them.

An adverse wind is a good wind as long as it comes from the direction in which the criminal is to be found, or in which he is running. Where there is a side wind more casting round is necessary. A whirlwind that seems to come from every side is not good.

A warm scent is one not more than two hours old; after that it is said to be cold.

In hot weather do not let the dog take up the trail in the middle of the day. Give the dog every opportunity from the commencement of this work to pick up the trail for himself, but take care that whilst engaged in this he does not come into contact with any other dogs.

If more Police dogs than one are to work the trail, take care that the dogs that are not working the trail at the time are not in a position to see the working dog. Again, in this case always be sure that the males take up the trail first, the bitches last.

Opening out the trail, lead the dog along—speak to him—encourage him to seek—let him have some clear, but not too cold, water to drink. Point to the ground and let him seek the scent—pacify him. Let him work slowly—take notice of his ears and his tail, by means of which you may observe when he is uncertain. Let him continue to seek the scent—

always pacify him again. Notice yourself, when he has unravelled the difficulties that puzzled him.

Should the dog lose the scent altogether go back in a slanting direction and let him start his work afresh. Again pacify him, and get him slowly and quietly to begin again, making use of some words that are familiar to help him—help him in the direction that he is to take.

Before and whilst engaged in this work the trainer should not take any alcoholic stimulant.

The dog's hunger should be appeased before starting work, but he must not be fed to satiety. If he has had a long journey he may be given a little milk in which a roll of bread has been soaked.

The journey to the scene of action should be taken without haste, and the best method is with a conveyance. The longer the journey has been the more necessary it is that the dog should be given an opportunity to rest and settle down before starting work. Care must be taken that the dog does not come into contact with tobacco smoke through travelling in a smoking compartment, or otherwise, as it will affect his olfactory organs.

6.—TESTS FOR THE DOG.

The qualities and accomplishments necessary to make a working Police dog may be briefly summarised as follows, and without these the animal should not be allowed to attempt criminal work:

1. Implicit obedience.
2. Undoubted courage.
3. To follow at heel and to act as leader whilst unleashed.
4. To bark at command.
5. To refuse food from a stranger's hand.
6. To fetch and carry, both out of water and over obstacles.
7. To jump at least 5 ft. high.
8. Perfect steadiness under gunfire.
9. To search premises and give tongue on finding person concealed.
10. To defend his master.
11. To follow up, throw down, hold fast, and give tongue.
12. To carry reports to the Police Station, or to an officer-in-charge.
13. By means of the scent, to discover and follow up a man's track. and search for stolen property.

7.—HINTS ON THE BREEDING AND REARING OF DOGS GENERALLY.

For the man ambitious of breeding and rearing his own dogs the following hints may be of use.

In the first place, relationship is to be avoided as much as possible. The evil consequences of in-breeding are now well known—the deficiencies of the bloodhound of to-day are due to this.

Also make sure that the bitch possesses good working qualities, as the puppies inherit her temperament. See she is a good feeder so as to make sure of having puppies with energy and vitality. To rear puppies that are poor eaters gives trouble without end. Observe well the bone, colour, shape and movement of the sire, as the puppies usually receive these from him.

Secondly, to breed from an old dog or bitch is improper, nor ought they to be suffered to breed till they are nearly two years old. March should be the mating season, when the whelps will have the advantage of the summer, and will have become sufficiently strong to withstand the rigours of a severe winter. The period of gestation is about 63 days, and from four to ten whelps are produced at a litter. If there is anything like the latter number, and it is desired to rear them all, recourse must be had to a foster-mother, as the whelps will be more than the dam can conveniently suckle herself. The young are brought forth blind, their eyelids being shut up with a membrane which comes off about the tenth day.

The whelps may be taken from the dam at five or six weeks old, or as soon as they will lap sufficiently. At this period the food given should be light, such as potatoes and milk, with a little oatmeal, etc. Puppies should seldom or never be indulged with carrion or flesh of any kind. Between the milk stage and adult diet there are puppy foods made by makers of repute which will be found to be all that is necessary. Care should be taken to see that the best biscuits are obtained, as inferior articles are sometimes offered for sale at a tempting price, but in such a case the meat will be found to be only on the surface instead of being incorporated with the farinaceous material of which the biscuit is chiefly composed.

If any of the whelps appear not to thrive a course of cod liver oil treatment will probably be beneficial.

At four months of age the puppies lose their teeth, which are quickly replaced by others, and are never afterwards changed. Now the food may be increased and the diet varied, though it will be sufficient if such food is given morning and evening instead of thrice a day as heretofore; and as the dog is carnivorous he should receive a certain allowance of meat, the amount dependent on the amount of exercise taken, or the work performed. Much meat without exercise will overheat the dog's blood, start him scratching, and very likely set up skin disease. A certain amount of vegetables helps to keep the blood pure, and also fish may be given occasionally. Oatmeal porridge with scraps from the table, or with a little gravy, makes another change, when, as sometimes happens, the dog gets tired of biscuits and even when hungry refuses to eat them, either dry or soaked.

In regard to the question whether dogs should be given bones to keep the teeth clean and promote the flow of saliva, the latest scientific theory is that this is all nonsense. As for the teeth, it is pointed out that tartar which constitutes dental uncleanliness, collects at the base, or neck of the teeth, where any rubbing process of bone, or biscuit, against tooth is impossible. Indeed, we are told bones are really tooth wearers, and that one need only look at the teeth of a dog habitually given to bone-gnawing, to be convinced that these organs would have been in a far better state of preservation had they not been so used. Referring to the saliva of the dog, it is said to be inert and has no digestive function whatever to perform, which is the exact opposite of the case in human beings, horses and cows. Thus, there is no need for a dog to masticate as there is for a human being, for it is the stomach and intestines that do all his digestive work. Be all this as it may, one must admit that dogs get much enjoyment from bone-gnawing, and that bones are a great help in keeping them amiable and contented. The bones should be of such a size that the animal cannot break them up and swallow the fragments, which are liable to become lodged in the throat, wedged between the teeth, or lacerate the walls of the stomach.

Although writers refer to " pups " of ten months, it does not mean the animal should be restricted to puppy foods up to that age. A period of adolescence sets in when he gets his second teeth, and he can take all adult food from now onwards to full maturity, which is reached short of two years. Fourteen years is the general period allotted for his life, but if he is kept to hard work every year he will seldom live so long.

Dogs of all ages should have access to good clean water. A dog can go all day without food and suffer little inconvenience, but requires a drink every few hours. The larger breeds should be fed twice a day, and the smaller ones three times.

Health without exercise is an impossible condition, and the pampered life permitted to so many of our canine pets, along with rich living, is responsible for permanent and fatal ailments. Young dogs should be tied up or confined as little as possible. It splays their feet and makes them bandy legged. The same effects in a less degree will be produced in a full-grown dog, which should have at least two hours' exercise daily, and not on a lead, but allowed his freedom to gallop and romp at will. In this connection, however, regard must be paid to feeding, neither exercise nor work being allowed immediately after a meal.

In regard to the conditions under which the dog should live, there are good firms that now make a speciality of their kennels for almost every breed of dog, and their lists should be consulted. In favourable weather the doors of the sleeping places should be left open day and night, as without plenty of pure air the dogs cannot thrive. Strict cleanliness and disinfection with a reliable disinfectant are necessary to keep away disease, and feeding and drinking utensils should be cleansed daily.

For bedding clean wheat straw is as good as anything, though if hay be used it should be sprinkled occasionally with disinfectants, as it is apt to harbour parasites. This bedding should be changed once a week.

Grooming with a brush in the direction of the lay of the hair should be done daily with a brush that is not too hard—never just after a meal, the evening after the day's work is over being the best time.

Dogs are liable to a somewhat formidable list of ailments with which it is not proposed to deal here, but many of these are due to want of cleanliness, insufficient exercise, injudicious or irregular feeding, and if the hints given are observed—ever bearing in mind that flesh food and idleness are the domesticated dog's worst enemies—the risk of disease will be much minimised, or if contracted will probably be in a mild form only.

The dog should be washed once a fortnight. Choose a fine day and wash him in the morning so as to avoid the risk of catching cold or inflammation by going to bed with a damp coat. Don't use a strong alkaline soap, nor ordinary soft soap. These destroy the gloss of the coat. The mildest of soaps which several reputable firms make as a speciality for dogs are the best. Always bear in mind that cold, damp and draughts are very injurious to a dog's health, and if a dog has to be exposed for some time to the wet without the power of running about and keeping warm he ought to have something to eat. Nearly all inflammations in dogs are caused by exposure to cold and wet whilst they are fasting.

TRAINING EXERCISES

PART I

The following training exercises show in detail the methods to be used for securing the requisites outlined in section 6.

1. The object of training exercises is to teach the young dog, which up to now has been attached to his master only out of selfishness, that he really has a master whom he always must keep in his eyes, whom he always must follow and obey. After the dog has reached the age of six months he has to be taken out into the street only in the leash; that is to say, he must learn to follow his master properly when in leash, and must be taught " street manners."

Carefully and slowly has the training to be started, the dog to be watched continuously and treated with great kindness in order to get to know all his capabilities, aptitudes and peculiarities. Great care must also be taken to avoid any haste, or to tire out the dog with over-exercise, and on no account has any exercise to be interrupted, otherwise the very foundation for future training may get undermined.

2. The exercise should be taken in an empty room or place surrounded with walls. If through necessity the exercise has to be performed in the open, a wall or close fence should be chosen; even a house which can be easily walked round will do at a pinch. People or other animals are never to be allowed to be present nor even to be seen.

3. The implements for training begin with training-leash and training-collar. If the dog is tender and sensitive, a training-collar without pricks had better be used.

Exercise 1.—First degree in " leash-walking." Word of command: " *Come*."

The object of this exercise is to teach the dog to be attentive to the trainer, to suppress all notions of sexual desires and other " doggy " bad habits. Then also to get him accustomed to his master's walk and step in order that later on he can follow without leash in the most populous and crowded places. The manner of teaching the dog: Go to the kennel, talk to the dog and let him out; conduct him into the exercise room, then put him on the training-collar in such a way that the pricks of the collar are on the top of the neck. Leash the dog and put the loop of the leash round your shoulders. In doing all this you are facing the door, whereas the dog stands in front of you facing to the right. This position is called the " Right Front Position." Then with the left hand get hold of the leash close to the neck. Say " Come," and turning right about you walk close to the wall so that your left hand nearly touches the wall. Naturally the dog now gets obstreperous and perhaps begins to whine, but no notice has to be taken. Without speaking a single word, you proceed along the wall three or four times round the room according to size. Owing to your having the leash in your left hand and close to the dog's neck he is bound to follow behind your left leg. You stop, talk, and pet your dog, and after a few seconds

17

repeat the order " *Come* " and go through the exercise as before. Never talk during the exercise. Should the dog lie down, then speak to him kindly until he gets up and follows; if he refuses, say "Come" and drag him along. The pain caused by the pricks in the training-collar will soon teach him to submit. After about ten minutes' exercise stop just at a time when the dog is doing well, stroke and pet him and take off the collar (all in the exercise room), and give your scholar a " tit-bit." Then play with the dog and make much of him until he has recovered from his astonishment or fright. Then take him back to the kennel, which he must not leave again all day.

Exercise·the dog during ten minutes in the mornings of five successive days and then proceed to the following exercise.

Note.—No dog should be exercised twice a day unless, perhaps, the morning exercise was less tiresome, when exceptionally he might be exercised a second time at nightfall.

Exercise 2.—Second degree in " leash-walking." Word of command: " *Come.* "

The object of this exercise is to teach the dog, which during the former exercise was forced on account of the wall to walk slowly behind your left leg, to follow and walk in the same manner when there is no obstacle to prevent his rushing forward. Method of teaching: Proceed as in Exercise No. 1 up to the word of command " Come," then turn and walk along the wall, your right hand nearly touching the wall. If the dog gets in front of your left leg, turn left about without saying a word and without stepping too hard on the dog's toes, because very little pain will teach the dog to understand that he is in the wrong place. Proceed, walking a little stretch with the wall touching your left hand, thus forcing the dog to keep his place as in Exercise No. 1. Turn again and keep the wall at your right-hand side, and as often as the dog gets in front of your left leg repeat the above manœuvre. Should the dog, feeling hurt, yelp or whine, do not take the slightest notice of it. Practise about a quarter of an hour on five successive days. After each practice take off the collar, give the dog a " tit-bit " in the exercise room, and when the dog has altogether quietened down, take him back into the kennel.

Exercise 3.—Third degree in " leash-walking." Word of command: " *Come.* "

The object of this exercise is to increase the dog's attention to the trainer, and to his movements. The close following behind the left leg gets more impressed on the dog's mind by making frequent turns to left and right.

Method: Put on the training-leash, go to the kennel and fasten collar to dog, and after the dog is quiet get hold of the leash in the prescribed manner (see Exercise 1), give the order " Come " and lead the dog into the exercising room, then go through the exercises of 1 and 2 for fifteen minutes. Repeat the exercise for five days. After exercise pet the dog, give him a " tit-bit " and take off the collar. After the dog has quietened down take him back into the kennel, where he must stay.

Note.—Should the dog be slow, find difficulty in the frequent change from right to left, get over-excited, then repeat for the first two days Exercise No. 1 only.

Exercise 4.—Fourth degree in " leash-walking." Word of command: " *Come.*"

Object of the exercise: The dog, which has by now learned to follow closely to the knee of the left leg, must learn to stick to his post under all conditions, whether the trainer walk slowly or fast, whether he turns to the left or the right, and whether he turns slowly or abruptly.

Method: Always fetch the dog out of the kennel in the prescribed manner (see Exercise 3). After the order " Come," walk to *middle* of exercising room, and walk fast and slowly alternately, turn now to the left, now to the right, now winding your way from left to right and vice-versa. Take great care that the dog keeps his nose to your left knee. If the dog transgresses, use the above-described means to remind him of his duties. Then after a few exercises along the wall, practise in centre of room. Practise for fifteen minutes and repeat on five successive days.

It is of the greatest importance that the dog should be proficient in these exercises.

Exercise 5.—Fifth degree in " leash-walking." Word of command: " *Come.*"

Object of the exercise: The dog, which has now learned to walk in the leash with his nose closely to the trainer's left knee when alone in a room far from human beings or other animals, has now to learn to do the same in the open.

Method: Fetch the dog with collar and leash as prescribed out of the kennel, and take him for a half-hour's walk. Walk in a straight line there and back in a quiet and little frequented street or place. Take the greatest care that the dog has his nose closely to your left knee and that you hold the leash as prescribed, because it must become the dog's second nature to be absolutely obedient, attentive and subject to you if you are to have success in future training exercises. After returning to the kennel take off the collar, pet the dog and give him the accustomed " tit-bit." Exercise one half-hour and repeat on three successive days.

Exercise 6.—Sixth degree in " leash-walking." Word of command: " *Come.*"

Object of exercise: To ensure perfection in " leash-walking."

Method: Take the dog from the kennel in the usual way and take him again for half an hour's walk in a quiet and unfrequented street or place, but change frequently your walking speed, now hurrying, now walking slowly, frequently turning right or left about. Always take the greatest care to hold leash in the left hand, and in the orthodox manner. Show disapproval of all faults the dog makes. If the dog is too hasty the best way to cure him is to turn quickly left about, and tread slightly on his toes. After finishing the exercise, take the dog back in the prescribed manner. Exercise for half an hour and for five successive days.

NOTE.—The dog leaves the kennel only for practice from Exercise 1 to end of Exercise 6. Exercise only during the forenoon, never at noontime when it is hot, nor shortly after feeding time. Be sure and bear in mind that the dog only knows the one word " Come," and thus do not expect him to obey any other call or whistling.

Exercise 7.—Last degree in "leash-walking." Word of command: "*Come.*"

The object of this exercise is to perfect the dog in leash-walking under all conditions.

Method: Fetch the dog as usual and take him for a walk through busy and crowded streets and thoroughfares. Watch that you hold the leash properly in the left hand, and that the dog's nose is in its proper place. After a while, select a quiet, unfrequented open place, pet the dog, make a great fuss of him, then take off the collar, and let him loose to jump and play about. Should the dog do anything wrong, do not call or whistle, nor shout, chide or punish him, as he knows only the one word "Come." Wait patiently until he comes, or call him in a pleasant and friendly manner by saying "Come," and return, after adjusting the collar and ordering "Come," in the usual manner to the kennel. Take such walks daily until the time of proper training has arrived.

Exercise 8.—Training to follow the scent.

The object of this exercise is to force the dog to use his nose, and to find his master by aid of the scent, and also to teach him at the same time that he should always keep his master in sight.

Method: This exercise is the same as No. 7, only choose a place for training where shrubs, holes, walls or hedges are handy for hiding purposes. As soon as the dog has started gambolling, hide yourself, but unobserved by the dog. Wait patiently in your hiding-place until the dog has found you, never mind how long it may be. The dog, as soon as he misses you, will anxiously look about, but, not seeing you, will rush to the place where he last noticed you, and not finding you there, will instinctively put his nose to the ground, trying to find you by the help of the scent. As soon as the dog has discovered you he will exhibit great joy, and equal joy must be feigned by you, and also make sure of having brought a "tit-bit" with which to reward him. Repeat this exercise during all your walks, always choosing a new hiding-place, but after about three days' practice it will be difficult for you to find a hiding-place, because by then the dog has learned by experience that he must keep his eyes on you permanently, even when at play.

Exercise 9.—Training the dog to bark inside the kennel when ordered. Word of command: "*Speak.*"

Object of exercise: To teach the dog to bark when ordered so that later on he will call and give signals, and the exercise is also a preparation for teaching the dog to call for assistance after discovering the wanted man, or to draw attention when meeting with something strange or suspicious.

Method: You start this exercise as soon as the dog has got accustomed to your daily walks, and is overjoyed when you approach him with leash and collar in hand. Enter the kennel, make a great fuss of the dog, and put on the collar, talking to him all the while. Suddenly take off the collar, and, leaving the dog behind, walk in the direction you are accustomed to take for your walks. The dog will get excited, and will start whining; then stop and call the dog, and almost without exception he will start barking. Stand still immediately; start praising him, saying, "Well done," " Nicely," " Speak." Return to the kennel, make much of him, and give him his well-earned " tit-bit," and whilst praising him put on the collar and start forthwith the daily walk. Next day, when approaching the kennel for the daily walk, give command, " Speak." If he does, praise him and reward him with a " tit-bit," put on the collar and take him for his walk. If he does not bark on command " Speak," repeat the word four or five times, and if he still refuses, repeat proceedings as described above until you succeed in getting him to bark on the word of command. Never omit to give the dog his " tit-bit " when earned, and do not forget to give him his walk. Another way of teaching a dog to bark on command is to put him with another dog already trained, and placing the two dogs side by side, order the trained dog to bark, after which pet and make a great fuss of him. Envy and the power of imitation will soon teach the other one to bark when told.

Exercise 10.—To bark in the exercise room. Word of command: " *Speak*."

This exercise will teach the dog after he has learnt to bark inside the kennel (because he wants to get out for his anticipated walk) that he must bark always on the command " Speak."

Method: Go to the kennel in the usual way, let the dog bark several times, put on the collar, and go into the exercise room; then take off the collar, and standing in front of the dog command " Speak." If he obeys the command, pet and reward the dog, put on his collar and take him for his walk. If the dog fails to respond, return slowly to the door, all the time ordering him to " speak." Finally leave the room, close the door, and order him to " speak." After a while knock at the door, commanding him to " speak," and as soon as he barks enter at once, pet and reward him, and after ordering him to " speak " again, put on his collar and take him for the accustomed walk. This exercise should be repeated until the dog barks at the first word of command inside the exercise room.

Exercise 11.—To bark in any room. Word of command: " *Speak*."

The object of this exercise is to make the dog understand that he has to bark, not because he gets rewarded, but because he has been ordered to do so.

Method: Take the dog out of the kennel in the usual way and into a barn, stable, living-room, or any other large but enclosed room, and proceed as in the last exercise. If the dog does not answer to the command " Speak," leave the room, when he is sure to respond. Afterwards pet him, but the " tit-bit " should be omitted, though, of course, he will get his walk. This exercise should be repeated until the dog responds to the command " Speak " in any room.

Exercise 12.—To bark in the open. Word of command: " *Speak*."

The object of this exercise is to make the dog perfect in responding to the command " Speak " and to make him understand still more that he must always obey.

Method: Let the dog bark first inside the kennel, then in the exercise room, after that in some other enclosed room, and take him for his walk to the place where he enjoys his usual gambolling; then standing in front of him you command " Speak." If he responds, pet him and let him romp about as usual. If, however, he does not respond, put on the collar and leave the place, return after a few minutes and again proceed as before.

Repeat this exercise until the dog responds to perfection in his accustomed place for romping and gambolling. Afterwards try him first in quiet and secluded but different places, and finally in places frequented by strangers. And do this until the dog obeys your command " Speak " anywhere.

Exercise 13.—To get the dog to bark on command and without commanding him when observing any suspicious object.

The object of this exercise is in the first place a primary lesson for such dogs as show reluctance to respond to the word of command " Speak " in the open. The other object of this exercise is to teach the dog to make use of his acquired ability, not only when ordered to " Speak," but also to use it as a means of communication with his master when he finds or perceives something strange, extraordinary or suspicious. In other words: This exercise is intended to be the foundation for the dog's sense of duty.

Method: In the open place, where you have often been hiding and where the dog had to find you, place a " dummy," and fasten to its right arm a string about eight yards long, then pass this string through a ring about a couple of feet above the dummy figure, and then lay the string in the direction you intend returning with the dog. Fetch the dog in the accustomed manner, but let him " speak " well, first inside the kennel, in the exercise room, and inside some other enclosed room as well. Then conduct him to the playground, and about 50 or 60 yards off the dummy figure take off the collar and start running towards the dummy. The dog will follow you and soon discover the figure, and as soon as he sees it give order, " Speak." If the dog is slow and stupid and does not respond, call him to you, speak to him kindly and pet him, then take hold of the string, and having drawn the dog's attention to the dummy figure, raise slowly the dummy's right arm. If the dog still remains mute, in spite of getting excited, as he will, order him to " Speak," and let him give plenty of tongue. Pet him, immediately after give him a " tit-bit," put on the collar and take him to some other ground for his daily gambol and romp.

This exercise has to be repeated often even after the dog has learned and freely gives voice (speaks) without command when finding the dummy.

NOTE.—To get the dog well grounded in the performance of his duty, practise with him daily, even after he has well learned all the lessons, but always be sure that he is punctual and prompt in the execution of all commands. Further, as often as possible let him accompany you, and try to get him accustomed to all kinds and all manners of surroundings, from the thronged thoroughfares of the noonday to the quietness and loneliness of the midnight street.

TRAINING EXERCISES

PART 2

It is now assumed that the dog has become proficient in the foregoing exercises, but it should be borne in mind that he must continually repeat what he has already learnt in order to remain fit and useful, because whatever he learns he must learn thoroughly. Here it may be useful to remark that on no account should he be trained to perform silly tricks, which only tax his nerves and bodily strength, but that his training should be confined entirely to the exercises as laid down. Before going on with the next part of the work it will be necessary to obtain the following training implements:

1. A straw whisk, 30 inches long, of which the middle part should be tightly bound to about the thickness of a man's wrist.

2. A block of wood for carrying purposes, with an arrangement at both ends for increasing or lessening the weight.

3. A leather bag for carrying purposes, and constructed in such a way that at both ends it can be weighted with shot or small stones.

4. Large old clasp knife.

5. Long line, 20 yards.

6. A stuffed dummy.

7. A movable boarding, 2 yards high and 1½ yards wide. The implements Nos. 1 to 6 lie in the training room, and the stuffed dummy figure should stand in a corner hidden behind the boarding.

The trainer and the dog should be fresh and vigorous when starting work, and all training proper should be done before feeding time. The trainer should fetch the dog for all training exercises out of the kennel by the line, and by the line take him back into the kennel, and should not remove the collar until by petting and praising he has quietened down the dog and regained his confidence. The trainer must give all commands or orders in such a low voice that the dog is forced to give all his attention to him. Every raising of the voice by the trainer should act upon the dog as a kind of correction and punishment. A short, sharp command should affect the dog like a hit with the whip, and make him obey instantly. Corporal punishment should never be administered unless the dog is held by the line and under absolute control. Really the trainer should not be satisfied until he is able to manage his dog by a scarcely audible whistling or by a slightly lisped " Pst." Each day that the dog has had a training lesson the trainer must take him for a walk during the afternoon, and after each training exercise and each walk the dog must be taken back into the kennel to quieten down there.

Exercise 1.—To teach the dog to sit. Word of command: " *Sit.*"

The object of this exercise is to teach the dog manners, and it will further be a preparation for future exercises, such as " lie down," " watch," " give up."

Method: Take a few walks with the dog round the exercise room, stop suddenly in the centre, turn left about, thus standing with the right side of the dog towards you. Take hold of the line with your right hand close to the collar, and place your left hand gently on the small of the dog's back, push him down with the left hand and slightly pull back his head with the right, at the same time giving the word of command " Sit." If the dog sits down, praise him and slowly stand up, but hold the line tight. If the dog tries to get up, give him a little jerk with the right, and gently press him down again with the left hand and order " Sit." When the dog stops sitting look at him, and with your index finger raised command " Sit." As soon as the dog sits still place yourself close to him in such a way that his toes are in line with the heels of your boots. After the dog has been sitting a few minutes, take a few turns round the room, stop again in the centre and repeat the exercise. Always take great care that the dog without turning or much moving promptly sits down and close to your left leg.

Exercise half an hour with two repetitions.

Exercise 2.—Word of command: " *Sit*," " *Stop*."

The object of this exercise is to get some groundwork for future exercises, and to get the dog thoroughly under control.

Method: Stop in the centre of the room and order " Sit." Step a little in front and face the dog, keep the line slack in your left hand, lift up your index finger and command " Stop," keeping your eye meanwhile on the dog. Take a step or two to the left. If the dog obeys and " stops," praise him. Go back to him and then take a few steps to the right, always ordering " Stop." Then proceed a little further off, and try to walk slowly round him, but keeping your eyes on the dog, the line in your left hand, and now and then order " Stop." After a while take another few turns round the room and start the exercise afresh. Finally walk round the sitting dog without repeating " Stop."

Exercise half an hour with five repetitions.

Exercise 3.—" Sit " and " Stop " without having hold of the line. Words of command: " *Sit*," " *Stop*."

The object of this exercise is to prepare the dog for learning to " sit " and " stop " without being fastened to the line and under all conditions.

Method: After having ordered the dog to " stop," drop the line and proceed to walk slowly round the dog, but keep your eyes on him. Pet him and show that you are pleased with his performance. Take a few turns with him round the room and repeat the exercise, but place the dog in such a position that he can see the entrance door. Then having walked around him a few times, walk slowly up to the door, stop short, walk quietly back to him, and a few times round him, pet and praise him, then treat him to a few turns round the room. Repeat the exercise, but when you have come to the door order " Stop " and leave the room, but watch through the keyhole to be ready to give orders to " Stop " in case the dog should become restless. After a short time re-enter the room slowly and unconcerned, and walk a few times round him. If the dog did well, pet and praise him, and reward him with a few more turns round the exercise room. During the remainder of the exercises stop outside the room up to about ten minutes.

Practice time, one half-hour, and five repetitions.

Exercise 4.—" Sit," " Stop," and " Come " when fastened to the line. Words of command: " *Sit*," " *Stop* " and " *Come* " and a low " whistling."

The object of this exercise is to train the dog to obey and come instantly when ordered " Come," or when called by whistling. *This exercise has to be practised thoroughly and completely mastered. It is absolutely necessary and of the greatest importance that the dog should give up following his quarry, and stop short in the attack when ordered " Come," or when whistled for.*

Method: Take the dog in leash into the middle of the exercise room and order " Sit," then change leash for line, order " Stop," and proceed close up to the wall. Now order " Come," and give a low whistle, and since the dog knows nothing yet of what he has to do, pull him gently by the line, repeating " Come," and also whistling. When the dog reaches you, pet and praise him. Take the customary turns round the exercise room, then repeat the exercise, and by the third day the dog should come like lightning. A short, sharp pull with the line will soon teach him and bring him to perfection. After the third day only order " Come " or whistle alternatively in order that the dog at your pleasure will obey either of them. Always give the orders and the whistle as low as possible, thus forcing the dog to give all his attention to you.

Exercise half an hour with three repetitions.

Exercise 5.—Practice of three first exercises in the open.

The object of this exercise is to prepare the dog properly for the real Police work by doing in the open what he has learnt to do between four walls and when alone.

Method: Take the dog to a secluded spot and repeat the Exercises 1, 2 and 3 in the ·same manner as in the exercise room. Increase the distances and, on and off, get into hiding for a short time, but never take your eyes off the dog, and also do not omit to treat him to a turn or two round the place between the exercises.

Exercise half an hour with five repetitions.

Exercise 6.—" Sit," " Stop," and " Come " when ordered " Come," or when whistled for in the open.

Method: Take the dog to a secluded place, take off the leash and put on the long line. Order the dog " Stop." Of course, you ordered him " Sit " before changing leash for line. Recede from the dog to distance of half a length of the line, and make the dog come alternatively by " Come " or by whistling. Be careful to give the order in a low voice, and if the dog does not come quickly, give a short, sharp pull with the line. After one or two exercises increase the distance to the full length of the line. On the second day take your distance both to the right and left of the dog, and on the third day behind the dog. Look well to sharpness in obeying the order " Come " or the whistling, and censure all shortcomings in that direction by a short, sharp pull with the line. *Amongst all your future exercises practise this one on and off, and do not yet let the dog do this exercise without having him on the line, as it might easily ruin his future training.* Directly the exercise is over take him back into his kennel and let him have his customary walk or romp during the afternoon.

Exercise half an hour with five repetitions.

Exercise 7.—To lie down in the exercise room.   Word of command:
" *Down.*"

The object of this exercise is to teach the dog perfect obedience to
his master, and it is at the same time the necessary preparation for the
" Creeping " exercise.

Method: Take the dog for a few turns round the exercise room,
then stop in the middle and order " Sit." Standing in front of him,
bend down and order " Down," and at the same time pull his front feet
forwards with your right hand, and with your left gently press down
his head in such a way that it lies flat between his paws, and leave him
in this position for a few minutes. Should the dog try to lift his head
give him a *slight* tap with a tiny cane or switch across his back, and order
" Down." After this to relieve him order " Come," and take a few turns
round the exercise room. Repeat as before, and when the dog lies down
and keeps still on command of the order " Down " alone, improve his
position so that his nose is exactly between his paws. Afterwards step
over the dog and walk round him, and always let him lie a few minutes
in the down position. As soon as the dog obeys perfectly to the command
" Down " commence lifting your right arm sharply when ordering
" Down," and afterwards give the command in a gradually lowering
voice, so that in the end the dog obeys and lies down when you give the
signal by your hand alone.

Exercise half an hour with five repetitions.

Exercise 8.—To lie down in the exercise room after the trainer leaves.

Method: As soon as the dog sits, order " Down " in a very low voice,
and at the same time quickly lift your right hand, holding the tiny cane.
If the dog hesitates, give him a slight stroke; after he lies down see that
he is in the right position with his head. Slacken the line and walk
round him, step over him and go right up to the wall, but always watch
the dog most closely and do not permit him to move ever so slightly.
Go as far as the door and finally leave the room, but watch him through
the spyhole. Return quietly and without any fuss, then walk up to the
dog, order " Come," pet and praise him, and take a few turns round
the exercise room. Again order " Sit," and repeat the whole of exercise.
Lower and lower give the command " Down " until it is a mere whisper,
but always with energy lift your right arm with cane in hand.

Exercise half an hour with three repetitions.

Exercise 9.—To lie down by signal inside the exercise room.

Method: Proceed as in the foregoing exercise, but after ordering
" Sit." No longer give the order by voice when wanting the dog to lie
down, but simply give the signal " Down " with the right arm, having
the cane in hand. Watch that the dog obeys promptly and keeps the
proper position.

Exercise half an hour with three repetitions.

Exercise 10.—To lie down whilst walking in the exercise room.

The object of this exercise is that the dog may learn to stop behind
when ordered and to bestow all his attention upon his master.

Method: Take a few turns round the room, stop suddenly and signal
and at the same time order " Down." Keep the dog down a few minutes,

and meanwhile walk round and step over him. Then order " Come "
and repeat the exercise, but only by signalling " Down " in the ordinary
way. Then change by ordering " Down " and signalling alternatively.
Walk quickly and watch that the dog goes " down " quickly.

Exercise half an hour with two repetitions.

Exercise 11.—To lie down by signal, then to come when called or whistled
for in the exercise room.

The object of this exercise is to teach the dog to watch his master
constantly and to be ready to obey order or signal promptly and without
any delay.

Method: After having changed the leash for the long line in the
exercise room, take a few turns round, then suddenly stop and raise
your right arm for " Stop," then recede a few paces and order " Come,"
but in a very low voice, and if the dog hesitates ever so little, give him
a short, sharp pull with the line. Repeat this, now ordering " Come "
and now whistling for him, and also changing your position from right
to left or from front to rear when giving the command. Give the short,
sharp pull with the line quickly after the command; the dog will not feel
it if he is prompt, if not it will punish him. If the dog does his work
well with quickness of execution, be sure and be lavish with your praise,
which will be found a great incentive.

Exercise half an hour with three repetitions.

Exercise 12.—To lie down on signal; to come when whistled for, then
down again on signal when given in the exercise room.

Method: Exercise with the dog as in No. 11, but when the dog is
in the act of obeying to the whistling for " Come " and has taken a few
leaps, suddenly lift your right arm and order " Down." Should the
dog not understand he has to lie down before he reaches you, give him
a slight hit with the cane and continue the exercise. After a while change
from ordering " Down " to signalling, and take plenty of turns round
the room between the single practices, otherwise the exercise will be too
fatiguing for the dog. If afterwards, that is, when the dog has been
fully trained, he should refuse or be slack in obeying either the command
or signal for " Down " put him on the collar and the long line, and let
him go through his exercise twenty times in succession, which will bring
him up to standard form for a long time after.

Exercise half an hour with five repetitions.

Exercise 13.—To lie down in the open.

Method: Take the dog to a secluded spot and repeat the Exercises
7 to 11. Watch that the "down" position is correct and give the order
more by signalling than speaking. Walk forward, then turn about, now
quickly, now slowly, or leisurely, and leave the line loose, but be ready
to use it for the short, sharp pull in case the dog is not prompt in the
execution of his duty. After exercise take the dog into his kennel, but
give him the customary walk during the afternoon.

Exercise half an hour with five repetitions.

Exercise 14.—To sit, to lie down, to come, then to lie down whilst coming, on the long line and in the open.

Method: This is to accustom the dog to perform in the open what has already been done in the exercise room under No. 12. Give all the commands, whether by speaking or whistling, very low. Let the commands and the pull at the line be almost simultaneous. Walk about and practise alternately.

Exercise half an hour with five repetitions.

Exercise 15.—To follow on the long line amongst obstacles.

The object of this exercise is to bring the dog to perfection in following his master without trouble when in line or leash.

Method: This exercise has to be taken where there are plenty of trees, posts, etc. Hold the line very loosely and run towards a tree or post in such a way as though you wished to pass it on the left, but in reality you pass it on the right, but get close to the tree or post with your left arm. If the dog out of carelessness or for convenience sake runs past the tree or post on the left side, he naturally gets a sharp pull by the collar, and thus a punishment. Do not stop yourself if the dog should be on the wrong side of the obstacle, and repeat this exercise frequently even days afterwards, as it will teach the dog to regulate all his movements according to yours.

Exercise half an hour with repetitions on and off at all times.

Exercise 16.—To lie down, then creep forward in the exercise room. Words of command: "*Down*" and "*Crouch.*"

The object of this exercise is twofold. In the first place it is a punishment without doing any harm, and secondly it completely brings the dog under obedience. To beat or thrash the dog makes him timid and shy, and more often than not spoils him. If later on the dog should do some mischief (for instance, if without having been ordered he attacked a man, cat, game or hens), here is the cure: Put on the training-collar and the long line, and make him creep round in circles for a distance of about 50 to 80 yards until he has reached the place where he committed his bad deed. After that he will never repeat the offence.

Method: Give order "Down" and having the line in your left hand the tiny cane in your right hand, give the order "Crouch," and at the same time pull the line with little jerks. If the dog tries to rise, give him a slight stroke with the cane, and at the same time order "Down" and continue step by step to make the dog crouch towards you. After a time give up repeating "Down," but give the dog a slight touch with the cane instead, and after about ten trials let him have a turn round the room, as this exercise is very exhausting.

Exercise half an hour with three repetitions.

Exercise 17.—To lie down and creep alongside his master inside the exercise room.

Method: Make the dog creep towards you as in Exercise 16, then walk backwards, step to the right side of his head, but take the line in your left hand. Change from right side to left side of head on and off, and whenever the dog tries to rise on to his legs give him a slight stroke with the cane. If he does well, show your satisfaction by praising him lavishly and do not omit the few walks round the room.

Exercise half an hour with three repetitions.

Exercise 18.—To lie down and creep when you are behind the dog and following him in the exercise room.

Method: Fasten the long line to the collar and pass it through a ring fastened to the floor as the end of the room and in front of the dog, then take the end of the line in your left hand and place yourself behind the dog. Now order " Down " and as soon as the dog is in proper position give the order " Crouch " and pull the line at the same time. If the dog grows restless because he cannot see you and tries to get up, give him a slight tap with the cane so that he understands that you can see him though he does not see you, and although not seen, his mistakes and disobedience get punished. After the dog creeps well when on the long line and through the ring, practise the exercise by holding him only with the leash, but always be ready to pull it sharply at any sign of disobedience.

Exercise half an hour with five repetitions.

Exercise 19.—To lie down and creep when free from leash or line inside the exercise room.

Method: Leave the dog with the collar on only and practise as in the foregoing exercise, but always stay behind the dog, and for every order badly executed put him on the long line. If the dog does well, let him only have one creep the length of the room. Immediately afterwards place yourself alongside the dog and order " Come," and let the dog follow you without leash or line. If the dog tries to be too much forward, step slightly on his toes and walk closely to the wall, your left arm touching it. At first only take straight walks, then make turns and twists. After a few turns about the room order " Down," step behind the dog and order " Crouch."

Exercise half an hour with five repetitions.

Exercise 20.—To creep in the open and when on line.

Method: Take the dog into a green meadow and drive your iron with the ring into the ground at some convenient place, pass the line through the ring, then exercise as in No. 18. Keep about a yard behind the dog and censure all shortcomings. If the dog does well, gradually slacken the line so that the dog begins to believe he is doing it without being tied to the line.

Exercise half an hour with five repetitions.

Exercise 21.—To creep in the open without line.

Method: Practise as in Exercise 19, but let the dog only creep about 15 yards, then after this do the same without the line, but every time he fails to obey or does bad work put him on the line, and a short, sharp pull accompanied by a slight stroke of the cane will soon teach him. During the afternoon walk let the dog run with the loose line, but, of course, in proper position.

Exercise half an hour with three repetitions.

Exercise 22.—Repetition of Exercises Nos. 1 to 14 inside the exercise room and without line.

Method: Go through all the exercises in the same order as the dog learnt them. Give the orders always in a low voice, and see that there is prompt obedience and correct execution. For any negligence the dog commits he must be put on the line. After a time vary the order of the exercises in all possible ways.

Exercise half an hour with five repetitions.

Exercise 23.—Repetition of Exercises Nos. 1 to 14 in the open and without being on the line.

Method: Practise exactly as in No. 22 and be as exacting as inside the exercise room, and do not hesitate to put the dog on the line whenever he makes a mistake.

Exercise one hour with five repetitions.

Exercise 24.—First exercise to teach carrying. Words of command: " *Fetch* " and " *Drop*."

Dogs are naturally inclined to fetch things back to their master, but that is only play, and should never be practised except as subsequently laid down, otherwise the dog will not turn out prompt and reliable, and will either drop the object anywhere, crush it or refuse to part with it at the critical moment. Throughout all the carrying exercises training-collar or cane must not be used for punishing the dog. Patience and repetition will alone lead to success. The object of this preliminary exercise for carrying is to teach the dog that the things he has to carry or fetch have to be touched carefully without doing any damage.

Method: After taking a few turns round the exercise room, stop short in the centre, order " Sit," drop the line, place yourself in front of the dog, and put your left hand over the dog's muzzle in such a fashion that your thumb and index finger enter the dog's mouth close behind the fangs on either side. With your right hand keep the dog's head horizontal and give the order " Fetch," and at same time press the dog's lips with your left thumb and index finger. Then as soon as the dog opens his mouth push your right hand, which must be gloved, quietly into it, and again order " Fetch." Continue to keep your left hand in its place, and your right one in the dog's mouth, and do not heed his struggles for freedom. Directly the dog is quiet with his head, give order " drop," and take your right hand out of the dog's mouth. Then be lavish with your praise and petting. Repeat the operation and try to keep your right hand longer in the dog's mouth, and try to get the dog to open his mouth promptly at the command " Drop," but wait for a moment when the dog is quiet before you order " Drop," and never forget to pet and praise him. After having done this about ten times, take a few turns round the room, and repeat the exercise. Watch that the dog opens his mouth promptly when ordered " Fetch," and if he does not understand his duty or refuses to do it, no other punishment must be administered except the slight pressure with the thumb and index finger of the left hand. Keep cool and do not show temper.

Exercise one hour with two repetitions.

Exercise 25.—Second preliminary exercise for carrying. Dog takes hold of the straw wisp. Words of command: *"Fetch," "Drop."*

The object of this exercise is to teach the dog to hold the object in his mouth without the trainer touching it.

Method: Stop in centre of room and drop the line, then step in front of the dog and order " Sit." Take the straw wisp in your right hand, placing your four fingers beneath the dog's lower jaw in such a way that the wisp lies close to the dog's mouth. Now order " Fetch " and push the wisp gently into his mouth, and if need be the left hand has to do the necessary pressing of the dog's lips behind the fangs. Leave your right hand under the dog's jaw and keep the wisp in the dog's mouth for a little time. After a while take away your right hand and let the dog hold the wisp unaided, but always order " Fetch." Try to step a little backwards and let the dog hold it for about three minutes, after which take hold of it yourself quietly and in a second or two order " Drop." Do not forget to pet and praise the dog. By degrees lengthen the time of holding the wisp, and carefully watch that the dog does not let go until he gets the order " Drop," and for this purpose touch the wisp now and then without ordering " Drop." Never omit, between the practices, to take the accustomed turns round the room.

Exercise one hour with two repetitions.

Exercise 26.—Third preliminary carrying exercise. The dog carries the straw wisp inside the exercise room. Words of command: *"Fetch," "Drop."*

The reason of this exercise is to teach the dog to carry objects.

Method: After the dog has taken hold of the wisp in the orthodox fashion and held it for a little while, get hold of the line with your left hand, and placing your right hand under his jaw, order " Come," and walk backwards, and as soon as the dog follows freely take away your right hand. Later on turn round and let the dog follow you in the proper way, *i.e.*, with his head close to your left knee. Watch the dog, and if he gives any sign of dropping the wisp, sharply order " Fetch " and pull the line slightly with your left hand, and with your right prevent him from opening his mouth. Order " Sit," wait for a while, then order " Drop," and at the same time take the wisp from his mouth.

Exercise one hour with two repetitions.

Exercise 27.—Fourth preliminary carrying exercise. The dog carries the wooden block inside the exercise room. Words of command: *"Fetch," "Drop."*

The reason of this exercise is to teach the dog to take hold of and carry a heavy object.

Method: Practise as in foregoing exercise. Carefully watch that the block lies in the dog's mouth behind the fangs, and thus the weight of the block will be less troublesome to him, and take special care that accidentally neither yourself nor the line jerk the block out of the dog's mouth. Little by little bring the weight of the block up to five pounds. Always take the usual turns round the room between the command " Fetch " and the order " Drop."

Exercise one hour with three repetitions.

Exercise 28.—Fifth preliminary carrying exercise. The dog carries inside the room the wisp, the block and the leather bag alternately. Words of command: *"Fetch," "Drop."*

The object of this exercise is to teach the dog to carry anything when ordered.

Method: Practise as in No. 26, and make the bag a little heavier at one end than the other.

Exercise one hour with one repetition.

Exercise 29.—Sixth preliminary carrying exercise. The dog obeys order " Down " in front of the wisp, takes hold and carries it. Words of command: *"Down," "Fetch," "Drop."*

This exercise is to teach the dog to pick up the object and carry it unaided.

Method: Place the wisp in the centre of the room and order " Down " about a yard in front of it. Take hold of the line with your left hand and with your right push the wisp towards the dog about half a yard, and at the same time order " Fetch " and slightly pull the line. As soon as the dog has taken hold, order " Come," take a few turns, order " Sit," and after a second or two " Drop." After a few turns round the room repeat the performance, and by degrees get the dog to take hold of the wisp when a yard from his mouth without pushing it towards him, and finally without your touching it.

Exercise one hour with two repetitions.

Exercise 30.—Seventh preliminary carrying exercise. The dog picks up the wisp, block and bag, and carries them alternately inside the room.

The object of this exercise is to teach the dog to pick up, carry and drop correctly any object.

Method: Practise with the wisp, block and bag, little weighted as in previous exercise, but watch that the dog takes hold of the objects in the middle, particularly the bag, and that they lie behind his fangs, and occasionally intermix some other exercise.

Exercise one hour with one repetition.

Exercise 31.—Eighth preliminary exercise for carrying. The dog, free from line or leash, brings the straw wisp on command. Words of command: *"Sit," "Fetch," "Here," "Drop."*

The object of this exercise is to teach the dog to pick up and fetch an object without first holding it, thus he will begin to understand that he must bring what he is told without mistake.

Method: Order " Sit," place yourself at the dog's side, and throw the wisp about a yard in front of the dog, wait a little, then order " Fetch," and at the same time bending forwards, point with your right hand towards the wisp. After the dog has taken hold of the wisp order " Here," pet him, order " Sit," and pet him again, and after letting him sit for a few minutes quietly take hold of the wisp, and after several moments order " Drop." Each time throw the wisp a little further and pause a little longer between the throwing and the ordering, but always order " Here " immediately the dog has hold of the wisp. Watch that the dog comes promptly and at once sits down, and never permit the dog to run round you before sitting down.

Exercise one hour with one repetition.

Exercise 32.—Ninth preliminary exercise for carrying. The dog has to bring and carry first the empty then the filled bag in the exercise room. Words of command: *"Fetch," "Drop."*

The object of this exercise is to teach the dog to fetch heavier objects and to pick them up and bring them quickly.

Method: Practise as in No. 30, and throw first the empty bag, after. that the bag equally weighted on both sides, and lastly unequally weighted. Do not bother about throwing the bag too far, but watch carefully that the dog picks up promptly and quickly returns. Always let the dog " Sit " with the filled bag in his mouth for a few minutes, and do not forget the pause between taking hold of the bag and ordering " Drop."

Exercise one hour with one repetition.

Exercise 33.—Tenth preliminary exercise for carrying. The dog, free from leash and line, brings different objects in the exercise room. Words of command: *"Fetch," "Drop."*

The object of this exercise is to train the dog to fetch and give up any object when ordered.

Method: Use for this exercise an old pistol or revolver, a piece of old chain, and an old pocket knife, but closed. Before you commence to throw any of these objects, first place them once or twice in the dog's mouth in the orthodox fashion. Let the dog fetch the objects in the " down " position first, then later on in the " sit " position. While going through this exercise it will be useful now and again to intermix some others with it, also off and on put your gloved hand into the dog's mouth to make sure he does not bite the objects when fetching and carrying them.

Exercise one hour with one repetition.

Exercise 34.—Eleventh preliminary exercise for carrying. The dog goes through the above exercises in the open. Words of command: *"Fetch," "Drop."*

The object of this exercise is to get the dog to fetch and carry objects in the open and under difficulties.

Method: Choose a lonely spot, an open meadow for preference. Repeat all the exercises from 24 to 33, first in the order the dog has learnt them, and then promiscuously, and watch for instant obedience. After a while give the order " Fetch," but do not wait for the dog's return; instead, turn round yourself quickly and run away as fast as you can. This will teach the dog to be as quick as he can. When the dog overtakes you stop at once, let him " sit," and pet him lavishly, and after a few minutes order " Drop." Later on when the dog overtakes you do not stop, but walk quietly on, allowing him to follow close to your left knee and carrying the object. Stop after a while and see that the dog " sits " at once, and always allow him to sit for a short time before you take the object.   After the exercise at once take the dog into his kennel.

Exercise one hour with two repetitions.

Excrcise 35.—Twelfth preliminary carrying exercise.   The dog learns in leash and inside the room to pick up with the greatest rapidity the straw wisp, the wooden block and the bag.   Words of command: *"Fetch," "Drop."*

The object of this exercise is to bring the dog to perfection in picking up lost objects like lightning in order to become absolutely reliable as a fetcher and carrier.

Method: Wrap some rags round the middle of the bag and the block so that the dog can get a better hold.   Fill the bag by degrees.   Place the wisp in the centre of the room and take a few turns round with the dog, slowly approach the wisp, and when near order " Fetch."   If the dog does not " fetch " talk sharply to him by saying " Shame," and showing your disgust in manner and voice, and giving him a pull with the leash.   Take a few more turns, and when again approaching the wisp order " Fetch," but let the leash go so that the dog can execute the command. When the dog has brought the wisp order " Sit," and pet him for his cleverness, let him " drop," then repeat the manœuvre. Always leave the leash loosely and get quicker in your movements until finally you run.   Afterwards practise with the wooden block, which you fill, and, little by little, make heavier, and lastly you do the same with the bag.   The last two days practise the exercise always running, as the dog must necessarily learn to pick up and bring all kinds of objects in the quickest manner and the shortest time, whether they are light or heavy.   Mix up a few other exercises with this and at the conclusion take the dog into his kennel immediately.

Exercise an hour with four repetitions.

Exercise 36.—Thirteenth preliminary carrying exercise.   The dog learns Exercise 35 in the open.   Words of command: *"Fetch," "Drop."*

The object of this exercise is to teach the dog to do on the line and in the open what he has already done in the exercise room without being distracted or influenced by any surrounding object.

Method: Practise the first day in a meadow and go through all the manœuvres as in No. 35.   Repeat on the second day, but on some rougher ground.   Work slowly and quickly alternately and frequently on the run. Give the orders in a low voice, and do not overlook any fault or negligence on the dog's part without punishment, which must, however, only consist of a short, sharp, but slight pull at the line.   The exercise should be repeated weekly later on in order to keep the dog in a properly trained condition.

Exercise an hour with two repetitions.

Exercise 37.—Fourteenth preliminary carrying exercise and also first exercise in high jumping. The dog practises fetching in the open and jumping over a boarding ½ yard high.   Words of command: *"Jump," "Fetch."*

The object of this exercise is to teach the dog when carrying objects to clear obstacles, if necessary, by jumping.

In a place adapted for the purpose erect two posts, two yards apart and one and a half yards high, and arrange them in such a way that you can raise the boarding between them in sections, that is by degrees, up to 1½ yards.

Method: Take the dog on the line, but held shortly, order " Come," then step over the boarding, ½ yard high, between the two posts, and when in the act of stepping over order "Jump." Repeat this a few times, then pass the posts on one side so closely that your left arm touches the right-hand post, order " Jump," and to ease the line pass it round the post by taking it with right hand out of left. If the dog understands his lesson and jumps willingly, let him perform without having him on the line. Afterwards place yourself in front of boarding, order " Sit," and throw the wisp over the boarding, and after a moment or two order "Jump," " Fetch," and step along with the dog on the line over the boarding. Then walk a few times over the boarding when the dog has the wisp in his mouth and following close to your left leg, each time repeating the order " Jump." Lastly order " Sit " and " Drop." Finally place yourself in front of the boarding, and the dog free from line gets the order " Sit." Then throw the wisp over and call out " Fetch," step close to the boarding but not over, and continually order " Fetch," make the dog jump back over the boarding and order " Sit " and " Drop." Repeat this exercise with the wooden block and by degrees increase the weight to 5 lbs. On the second day let the dog clear the boarding with the weighted block and bag. Take a few turns round the place, order " Sit " and " Stop," and meanwhile increase the height of the boarding by adding another board. First let the dog clear the increased height without object, then with object, light, and finally weighted. After the dog has learnt to jump the obstacle with ease, go on increasing the height up to 1½ yards. Allow the dog at times to get hold of your hand to remind him he must neither bite nor crush the objects he has to carry.

Exercise an hour with three repetitions.

Exercise 38.—Fifteenth preliminary carrying exercise and exercise for flat
        jumping. The dog carries object across a ditch. Word of
        command: " Fetch."

The object of this exercise is to teach the dog to clear holes and ditches of considerable width when carrying some object.

Method: Take the dog on the slackened line and with him jump a ditch about a yard wide. Repeat this a few times, then throw the wisp, but not across the ditch, order " Fetch," and when the dog has brought it order " Sit " and " Stop," cross the ditch by yourself, and walking on the other side, order " Come " or whistle, and as soon as the dog has reached you, stop and show your satisfaction by praising him, and finally order " Drop." Repeat this exercise with block and bag, and increase their weight. If the dog does all this well, then approach the ditch and throw the wisp across, but the dog must see you do it. Order " Fetch," and repeat with block and bag. After this place the wisp on one side of the ditch and with the dog cross to the other side, and pointing with your hand towards the wisp, order " Fetch." If the dog does not do it, cross with him to fetch it and repeat until he understands. Practise then with block and bag in the same way and gradually increase their weight and also by degrees, increase the distance between you and the ditch to about fifty yards.

Exercise an hour with three repetitions.

Exercise 39.—Sixteenth carrying exercise. First exercise for finding lost objects. The dog seeks and fetches objects his master has lost. Words of command: *"Lost," "Fetch."*

The object of this exercise is to teach the dog to make use of his nose by following his master's track, and thus find the lost object.

Method: Take the dog into an open but quiet place, which you can easily overlook from high ground, but which has obstacles, such as ditches, holes, walls, trees, bushes, etc. Let the dog first " fetch " a selection of different things, which you as a rule carry about with you, thus being affected with your scent; for example, gloves, bunch of keys, knife, purse, etc. Let the dog fetch these without being on the line. After a while, whilst walking, drop one of the objects the dog has previously fetched, though the dog must see you drop it. Continue walking for about ten yards, then turn round with the dog, bend down, point with your hand on your track, and order " Lost," " Fetch." Repeat this a few times, and then after having ordered " Lost," " Fetch," turn round and walk away so that the dog must follow you with the " fetched " object in his mouth. Increase the distances by degrees; change the objects, and finally drop them without being noticed by the dog. On the second day, when taking the dog out of his kennel, drop some object just outside, and walk on about 100 yards, then order " Lost," " Fetch," but don't wait for the dog. Then on some covered ground let him fetch lost objects from any distance up to 500 yards, but no longer walk in a straight line, but take curves, and make twists, go through bushes, round walls, and jump over ditches. Make the dog follow you in the orthodox way and carrying the lost object in his mouth. On the third and succeeding days take the dog from the kennel, first into the house, and drop some object just outside the door, and later on inside the passage, and order " Lost," " Fetch," as on previous days. Repeat the exercise, but always under more difficult circumstances until finally he has to fetch the object about a mile. Practise this exercise in after days, and on all your walks, and make it a special practice to leave something inside the passage of your house, and when giving the order " Fetch," always be sure to bend down and point conspicuously to the ground, saying first " Lost."

Exercise an hour with five repetitions.

Exercise 40.—Seventeenth carrying exercise. The dog has to find and carry the heavy block and bag. Words of command: *"Lost," "Fetch."*

The reason for this exercise is to get the dog to carry heavy objects for long distances.

Method: Order " Sit " and " Stop," walk away, then return in a circle to the dog, but on the way drop the heavy block, then order " Lost," " Fetch," but make the dog follow your track the way you came back, in order that he may begin his nosework where the scent is freshest. Walk away, and after the dog has reached you, he must follow in the orthodox fashion for about fifteen minutes, with the heavy block in his mouth.

Exercise an hour with one repetition.

Exercise 41.—Eighteenth carrying exercise. The dog seeks and fetches objects belonging to his master which have been buried. Words of command: " *Lost*," " *Fetch*."

The object of this exercise is to teach the dog to seek and find his master's objects buried somewhere in his track, and to make him more alert, and careful in using his nose.

Method: Choose a place well covered with trees, bushes, holes, ditches, etc.; order the dog " Sit " or " Down," and retire, but not more than 20 yards, and hide some personally-worn object which the dog has fetched before behind some bush, or in a hole, but on your track, cover it with some moss or sand, and then return to the dog in a short circle. Show the dog the scent carefully, and order " Lost," " Fetch," but let him go the way you returned, and not in the direction you went. Continue the exercise, and each time make the distance a little further, and bury the object a little deeper, up to 30 inches. Lastly choose some bush and pass through it and over it repeatedly, then bury the object therein, but restore the appearance of the bush as it was before you touched it, and let the dog then fetch the object. Be lavish with your praise, and repeat the exercise continually, and always under greater difficulties.

Exercise an hour with three repetitions.

Exercise 42.—Nineteenth carrying exercise. The dog finds and fetches objects belonging to a stranger. Words of command: " *Lost*," " *Fetch*."

The object of this exercise is to teach the dog, by means of the scent, to find the objects of strangers, whether lost, hidden, or thrown away. This exercise will at the same time be a valuable preparation for training the dog to recognise by means of the scent, criminals and stolen objects.

Method: Your necessary assistant has to be on the exercise ground before you, and you meet him there. He hands you one of his personal objects, such as a glove, handkerchief, etc., and you let the dog fetch it several times, then the assistant takes the object back, and goes about twenty yards off, and drops it, so that the dog can see it done, but, proceeding, he must hide behind something. When he is out of sight, press the dog's nose slightly on the assistant's track so that he must scent it, and showing him the direction, order " Lost," " Fetch "; if the dog refuses go with him and praise him much after he has picked it up, then order him " Sit," holding the object in his mouth, and finally " Drop." Take care that the assistant never crosses his own previous track, that he always disappears before you give the order to the dog, and perform the exercise on some ground where you can follow by sight the track of the assistant, thus enabling you to correct the dog should he make a mistake, or get mixed. Under no circumstances must an occasion arise where the dog cannot find the object. After a while the assistant may change from a straight line to a zig-zag one, and may increase the distances. You yourself should never leave the place where the dog was ordered " Lost," " Fetch," until he returns with the object to you, unless it is really necessary to assist the dog.

Exercise an hour with five repetitions.

Exercise 43.—Principal carrying exercise. The dog has to seek, find, and fetch objects buried by an assistant. Words of command: " *Lost*," " *Fetch*."

The object of this exercise is to increase the dog's reliance on his nose, and to make him less dependent on his master when doing " nose-work," thus getting him ready for real criminal work.

Method: The assistant hands you some of his personal objects and you let the dog " fetch " them. Practise as in No. 41, but with this alteration, that you stop, and the assistant proceeds, and buries one of the objects. Repeat this a few times in succession. Then let the assistant bury the object in some shrubbery, and run through it in all directions, backwards and forwards, both to right and left, but the place where the object was buried must have no outward sign of disturbance. After the assistant has vanished, order " Lost," " Fetch," but showing the dog carefully the assistant's track. On future days exercise this often in order to keep the dog in practice.

Exercise an hour with three repetitions.

Exercise 44.—Bringing in reports on the training ground. Words of command: " *Report*," " *Back*."

The object of this exercise is to train the dog to take a message.

Method: Exercises 42 and 43 have been of value in preparing for this, and they should be borne in mind. Choose your training ground close to some bushy underwood, the ground itself being open and unfrequented. Order your assistant to select an old pair of his gloves, and to arrive on the ground with them on. Take a glove, and let the dog fetch it a few times; return it to the assistant, and let him go away about 50 yards, carrying the glove swinging in his hand, in order that the dog can see it, and you must besides draw the dog's attention to it all the time the assistant has it in his hand. Order " Sit," and after a minute or so order " Report," " Lost," " Fetch," and pointing towards the assistant you let the dog go. The dog, eager to fetch the glove, comes up to the assistant, who orders him " Sit," praises him, and giving him the glove, orders " Back." When the dog returns you order him " Sit," and make a great fuss of him, then order " Drop," and take the glove from him. Exercise in this manner a few times. After a while order " Sit," and put the letter bag on the dog, and with great ostentation place a piece of paper into it, and order " Report," pointing at the same time towards the 50 yards distant assistant, who awaits him, orders " Sit," and puts on the line, then praises him, opens the letter bag, and takes out the paper and examines it. After giving a "tit-bit" to the dog, he ostentatiously replaces the paper in the letter bag, loosens the line, and pointing towards you, he orders " Back." On the second day increase the distance, but the assistant must never be out of sight. On the third day let the assistant enter the bush, first 50 yards, then up to 100 yards, and finally up to 300 yards. In later exercises let the assistant get away up to about a mile. Never over-exercise the dog, and a long-distance report should be made only once on each day. Repeat this exercise during night, but take special care that the assistant separates from you in the open, in order to give the dog a better chance to pick up his scent. Increase the time between the assistant leaving you and the order " Report " by degrees up to three-quarters of an hour.

Five repetitions.

Exercise 45.—Taking reports to the Police Station. Words of command: " *Station*," " *Back*."

The object of this exercise is to teach the dog to run for assistance to the Police Station.

Method: Don't lose sight of the experience you have gained during the practice of Exercise 44. Send the assistant to the Police Station, and thither you must proceed with your dog as well. When there the assistant should make a fuss of the dog; then you leave, and the assistant accompanies you as far as the door, and stops there; you continue about 50 or 60 yards, then order " Sit," and put on a letter bag, and write out a message and place it in the bag; all of which should be done with considerable show, in order to draw the dog's attention to it, after which, pointing towards the Police Station, order " Station." The dog, under the influence of the late exercises, and knowing the assistant is there, quickly obeys. The assistant puts him on the line, makes a great fuss of him, and takes him into the office (the same room must be always used, and the dog always taken into it), orders " Sit," and pretending great excitement opens the letter bag, takes out the message, and gives the dog a " tit-bit." He then replaces the paper in the bag, takes the dog to the door, undoes the line, and pointing towards you, orders " Back." As soon as the dog reaches you order " Sit," and praise him, open the bag and take out the message. Give the order " Come," and repeat the exercise from about 100 yards, with the assistant leaving the door open, and awaiting the dog in the passage. With the next repetition increase the distance, and let the assistant await the dog inside the inner office door. In performing this exercise always first give the order " Sit," and always be careful to take out the message from the bag with great ceremony, after which pet and reward with " tit-bit," as this gives the dog the impression that the taking of the paper or other object from the bag is the principal thing. On the second day increase the distance to 300 yards, and on the third day start your practice without the assistant being present at the Station, so that he has not seen or petted the dog before you have set out, only instruct him to be there ready to receive the dog when he arrives, and begin this at a distance of 50 yards, which gradually increase, and finally go to some place in a different direction from which the dog has yet set off for the Station.

Time of Exercise: About three or four practices of order " Station," " Back," daily, with five repetitions.

Exercise 46.—Taking reports to the Police Station with the door closed, and the dog announcing his arrival by barking. Words of command: " *Station*," " *Back*."

The object of this exercise is to enable the dog to make his presence known and save time.

Method: Go to the Station with the assistant and the dog, the latter on the line. At the entrance door take off the line, order " Sit " and " Stop," then with the assistant enter and shut the door. After a few minutes open the door a little, order " Come " or whistle, but shut the door at once, leaving the dog outside, and when he starts whining or scratching at the door, order " Speak," and the systematically-trained dog will give tongue at once. Let him bark for about five minutes, continually ordering him " Speak." After this you go inside the room where the dog is always received, and the assistant now opens the outer door for the dog to enter and follows him to the closed door of the room wherein you are, and orders him " Speak." Let him speak under the encouragement of the assistant for another five minutes, then open the door yourself, make a great fuss of the dog, and give him a " tit-bit." Repeat a few times. After a while leave with the dog, and return to the Police Station in a roundabout way, the door is shut, and behind it stands the assistant. Knock at the door, and shake it, all the time ordering " Speak." After about five minutes have the door opened from the inside, not by the assistant this time, but by another Policeman, who inside rewards the dog with a " tit-bit " and plenty of petting. Repeat until the dog has mastered the lesson well. On the second day you practise as on the first with the exception that you do not accompany the dog, but send him with the letter bag, and he is received at the entrance door by the assistant, who puts him on the line, and goes with him to the door of the receiving-room, which must be closed, shakes it, and orders " Speak." Then immediately the door must be opened, the dog instructed to " Sit," whilst the message gets taken out of the letter bag, and, patting and " tit-bit " business over, the message is replaced and the dog gets the order " Back." Next the entrance door is closed, with assistant behind it, and if the dog whines or scratches, he orders " Speak," and immediately opens the door, puts the dog on the line, and lets him speak again at the inner door, opens at once, and proceeds as before. This exercise must be repeated until the dog freely announces his arrival at the closed door.

On the third day increase the distance up to 200 yards.

Three repetitions.

Exercise 47.—Taking reports to the Police Station, announcing his presence at closed door by barking, and allowing other officers to receive the message. Words of command: " *Station*," " *Back*."

The object of this exercise is to teach the dog that anybody in the office has a right to receive his message, and return an answer.

Method: The entrance door of the Police Station is shut, and the assistant absent, but behind the door another officer stands waiting. Take the dog to the same place from where he first took the message to the Station, give the order " Station," and as soon as the dog gives tongue at the outer door, the officer should at once open it, let in the dog, shut the door, then open the door of the inner office, also closing that one after the dog has entered. The officer then orders " Sit," and with much ado extracts the message, lavishly praises the dog, and rewards him with a " tit-bit," and afterwards the return message is, also with great show, placed in the letter-bag, the doors opened and the dog ordered " Back." Henceforth the dog should not be put on the line when arriving at a Station. Practise this exercise from different places, and each time a little further distant from the Police Station.

NOTE.—After three repetitions on three successive days, practise this exercise frequently during both day and night, but always take care the dog is promptly received, the paper extracted, and, after a few minutes, replaced with considerable ceremony which the dog should observe, and the " tit-bit " must not be omitted. Lastly, you must no longer wait on the spot from whence you sent the message, but proceed on your beat, and the dog, as he has already learned to do, will seek and find you.

Exercise 48.—Guarding objects. Word of command: " *Rest*."

The object of this exercise is to teach the dog to lie down on command, and to stop there, until his master personally fetches him. Thus, when necessary, he will be able to watch objects, and not allow strangers to touch them. On no consideration must the dog quit his post, whether strangers whistle, call, or in other ways try to entice him, and not even when his own master calls or whistles, but only when he comes personally. This exercise will likewise serve as a preparation for training the dog to watch, and take care of prisoners.

Method: For practising the exercise choose a place where it will be possible for you to approach the dog under cover, and unobserved. Take the line off the dog, and from your shoulders, roll it up, place it on the ground, and, pointing to it, order " Rest," and at the same time push the dog quietly and gently on to the ground, in such a way that the line lies close in front of him. The dog must keep his head up so that he can watch better all round. Now walk backwards a little, but keep your eye on the dog, and should he try to get up and follow, threaten him with your finger, and order " Rest." Walk round the dog, but continue ordering " Rest." After a while, with your head turned away, whistle; if the dog leaves his place, call out at once " Down " and with disgust, " Shame," and, shortly after, " Rest." Make him creep by ordering " Crouch " to the place he had left, lift up the line, then, dropping it, order " Rest." Repeat this, but henceforth, make larger circles round the dog, and talk to yourself, also call and whistle, and after having had to creep back a few times the dog will get to know what is expected of him. After the dog has got so far advanced that he will not quit the object, whether you call or whistle, contrive to disappear suddenly, then unseen by the dog, creep up near to him, so that you can see and watch him unobserved. When the dog gets up to look for, or follow you, call out sharply " Shame," and order " Rest "; and if he has left the spot, order " Down " and " Crouch," making him creep back, meanwhile administering a slight stroke or two. When he has crept back, lift up the line, order " Rest," and drop the line in front of him. After this make a few more circles around the dog, disappear once more, and repeat as above, but as soon as the dog becomes restless, whistle for him; if he follows, turn to him with " Shame " and make him creep back. After the dog has learned to stop quietly ten minutes, then fetch him, but never praise the dog; simply approach, take up the object, and order " Come." If you are able to use the catapult accurately, you may make use of it, and, when he tries to get up and leave the object, hit him with a small stone or bullet, a proceeding that will ensure swifter progress.

Exercise one hour with two or three repetitions, according to success. Afterwards practise the exercise in your afternoon walks until the dog will rest quietly for at least an hour.

Exercise 49.—Guarding objects. The " resting " dog does not quit his charge at the bidding of the assistant. Word of command: " Rest."

The object of this exercise is to teach the dog that he must stop with the entrusted object until his master personally calls for it.

Method: Go to the same training ground as in Exercise 48, and take the assistant with you, loose the dog, and after giving the order " Rest," proceed with the assistant some distance away. In a half-circle the assistant returns to within a few yards of the dog; meanwhile, you get into hiding and creep close up. The assistant then calls the dog, and if he does not leave his charge should not be tempted by him too long for the first time, neither should he come too near the dog, or under any circumstances touch him; after this you come forward and take hold of the charge. If, however, the dog leaves his charge and goes to the assistant, you at once disclose yourself and show your disapproval by calling out sharply " Shame," " Rest," and, after putting him on the line, he must crouch back in a circle, receiving in doing so a few slight strokes with the cane, and repeat the exercise. After the dog has so far learnt this lesson, commence walking and running past him alone, and in company with the assistant, whistling and calling alternately, until the dog fully understands that on no account must he leave the object he is guarding until you personally come for it.

Exercise one hour with one repetition, but repeat later on at times in order to keep the dog well posted in his duties.

Exercise 50.—To teach the dog to refuse food from anyone but his master when " resting." Word of command: " *Rest.*"

The object of this exercise is to teach the dog to refuse food from strangers, so as not to be enticed to give up his charge, and to avoid being poisoned.

Method: Take an assistant whom the dog has never seen, and who is wearing no Police uniform of any kind. Keep the dog on the line, order " Rest," fasten the line to some post or tree, go about 20 yards sideways from the dog, and let the assistant approach from the opposite side to within five yards of the dog, which he should call and then show him a piece of meat, but on the dog approaching to take it the assistant pulls back the meat and gives the dog a sharp stroke with the cane. Afterwards let the assistant throw the piece of meat just within reach of the dog, and if the dog tries to take it he again hits him with the cane, then you turn up and order the dog to " Speak," letting him give plenty of tongue; meanwhile, the assistant surreptitiously offers the dog the meat, but whenever the dog attempts to take hold of it lands him one with the cane for his trouble. Go on in this way until the dog will not look at the meat any more. At the conclusion the assistant should take the meat away with him, and under no consideration must the dog be allowed to have it.

Exercise *ad libitum* according to the measure of success, and repeat frequently, but always change the assistant.

Exercise 51.—The dog gives tongue in the open at the sight of the dummy. Words of command: *"Go," "Speak."*

The object of this exercise is to prepare the dog so that he will give tongue when he encounters the criminal, missing person, or lost object until his master arrives.

Method: Place the dummy amongst some shrubbery and approach it with the dog on the line in such a way that you do not notice it until you are within a few paces, when, pointing towards it, you order " Go," " Speak." Whilst the dog is giving tongue you walk round the dummy, then retreat a few steps, but if the dog attempts to follow you, order " Go," and continually let him give tongue. He must be taught to stop with the dummy, and must not touch it whilst you go away. Don't allow the dog to go through this fatiguing exercise for more than five minutes, after which return to him, with praise, and a " tit-bit," and continue your walk. When the dog has recovered from his fatigue return with him to the dummy, but this time in such a way that you can both see it when you are fifteen yards away, then, pointing towards it, give the order, " Go," " Speak," and retire some distance away, but so that the dog can always see you, and if he should stop barking order " Speak."

After about five minutes go to the dog, pet and reward him, and proceed with your walk. On the third trial free the dog from the line when within twenty-five yards of the dummy, and order " Go," " Speak." Should the dog not understand advance a few steps with him, but stop as soon as he does understand, and obeys the order. Three practices of five minutes' duration within the hour are sufficient. On the second day place the dummy near the same spot, but noticeable from a distance, and when you are within twenty yards show it to the dog, ordering " Go," " Speak." If the dog does not go at once, take a few yards alongside and encourage him, but stop as soon as he understands what you mean. If the dog gives tongue well, retire about ten yards, but so that he can see you, and always order " Speak " when the dog begins to flag. After five minutes approach the dog, praise and reward him, and proceed with your walk. Repeat this performance, but increase your distance after the order " Go," " Speak," has been given and obeyed, and you may let the dog give tongue a little longer than five minutes, but then you must give him some food. On the third day place the dummy in the same conspicuous position, and when within twenty yards give the order " Go," " Speak," then watch him closely from behind some tree or other object, but so that he cannot observe you. This time let him give tongue for about eight minutes, afterwards being lavish with your praise and rewarding him generously. The next time do as before, but give the order when about 50 yards distant, and don't forget to order " Speak " whenever the dog gives up barking, and the third time increase the distance still more. If the dog now refuses to obey be very patient, and do not speak loudly or harshly to him; in fact, it will be better to start again from the beginning of the exercise and repeat more often. In order that the dog may grow to like this exercise and look forward to it, make him understand there is always a good " tit-bit " when performed to your satisfaction.

Exercise one hour with three repetitions.

Exercise 52.—The dog as leader to his master. Word of command: " Front."

The object of this exercise is to teach the dog to walk in front of his master in order to discover persons hiding anywhere near.

Method: First bear in mind that this exercise is only to be used when on roads, or in the street, elsewhere the dog should follow close to your left knee, unless he is seeking round anywhere on being ordered to do so. Choose a lonely road, and let the dog follow you on the loose line. Suddenly step aside a little and, ordering " Front," try to get behind the dog. The dog, of course, having been accustomed to walk behind you, will find it difficult to know what you mean, therefore repeat the order " Front," point forwards and pretend to throw something in front of him. After the dog understands what you mean, and has walked in front a few minutes, let him follow you again for a while. Repeat this for some time. If you come across some pedestrians, whistle for the dog, but very low, and order " Come." After the dog has learnt on the line that he must be in front only a few yards, then practise with him loose. Lastly, after you have got the dog to obey the order " Front " instantly, start suddenly to turn in another direction, but don't call or whistle for the dog at all, but when he comes pet him freely, turn round about, and continue in your original direction; never call or whistle for him when you do this, though always pet and praise him when he comes, thus the dog will acquire the habit of paying permanent attention to you, even when in the execution of his duty. Practise this also during the night time, first on straight roads, then by taking suddenly to side streets, or returning.

Exercise frequently and particularly during the night.

Exercise 53.—The dog follows a ten-minutes-old scent after smelling some article belonging to the assistant and gives tongue on finding the dummy behind which the assistant is hiding. Words of command: " *Follow,*" " *Find.*"

The object of this exercise is to prepare the dog for criminal work by teaching him to follow a specific scent and to give tongue when finding his quarry.

Method: Bear in mind that in this exercise the dog must always succeed in the practice so that he gains perfect reliance in his nose-work, and on no consideration has the dog to find his quarry either by sight or hearing. In this exercise put in a good stock of patience, act calmly, and never lose self-control, but be content if the dog is able to do good work after a few months, for it will take years to make him really perfect. Never take an assistant in uniform during this practice, but make use of the old assistant whose scent is already familiar to the dog. Order this assistant to leave one of his old gloves, and one used on that day at a certain spot, and proceeding, hide with his dummy about 50 yards further on, by standing behind the dummy in such a manner that he is unseen. If the dog moves from one side to the other the assistant must always contrive to have the dummy between himself and the dog. You should approach the place where the glove is lying from a different direction to that taken by the assistant. Order the dog, which is on the line, " Sit," and show him the glove; let him sniff well at it, then. placing yourself astride the dog, show him the track, and push his head gently on to it, and show him thus for a few feet, or yards if need be, then loose him, point forward with your hand, and order " Follow." You follow on slowly, and if without being ordered the dog gives tongue on reaching the dummy, approach within twenty-five yards, praise him and encourage him to continue barking by frequently ordering " Speak." If the dog returns order " Go," " Speak " and make him return to the dummy. The assistant should now and then move one of the arms of the dummy, or move it altogether a little, but on no account must he make any movement that smacks of attacking the dog, or striking at him, and also see that the dog never gets hold of the dummy. Should the dog, however, touch the dummy call " Shame," put him on the line, and place yourself five yards in front of the dummy, ordering " Speak," and walk round the dummy. After the dog has given tongue well, approach, pet and reward him well, and give him a chance to recuperate by taking a short walk. In exactly half an hour's time, and when you are out of sight, the assistant should take the dummy to another place, about 100 yards away, walking in a tortuous line and leaving on the old spot one of his personal articles. After the assistant has been gone about ten minutes you arrive at the spot, and you let him seek on the line until he has found and " fetched " the article left by the assistant. Let the dog sniff well, then, bending down, show him the scent carefully and patiently for a few feet, loose him, point in the direction the assistant went, and order " Follow," and observe the dog follows the serpentine scent, and follow slowly behind him. As soon as the dog arrives in front of the dummy, the assistant should move one of the arms, but stop on the spot and always turn in such a way that the dummy is invariably between him and the dog. Proceed as before, and after about ten minutes, put the dog on the line and leave the place. For the third practice let the distance be 150 yards, and the walking of a zig-zag nature. Practise as before for about ten minutes, then praise and reward the dog. On the second day practise with an assistant little known to the dog, choose other hiding places, and repeat as before. On the third day take an assistant totally strange to the dog, thus teaching him to perform the exercise regardless of whose scent it is.

Three repetitions.

Exercise 54.—The dog follows the new scent—20 minutes old—and gives tongue when finding the assistant (without dummy). Words of command: *"Follow," "Find."*

The object of this exercise is to teach the dog not only to follow somebody's scent, but also to give tongue when finding them, and without being enticed thereto by the dummy.

Method: Instruct the assistant to leave a pre-arranged spot at a given time and walk in curves to another place about 150 yards distant, and to leave some personal object on his own track at that distance, then to lie on the ground hidden close by. You yourself act as prescribed in Exercise 52. If the dog gives tongue when he has reached the assistant, the assistant should lie still where he is, if not, then he had better first sit up, and if need be, move his body a little, but on no account assume a threatening attitude. After the dog has given tongue for about ten minutes, praise and reward him and finish the exercise. For the second practice let the assistant go the same distance, but walk there in some right angles. For the third exercise let the assistant's track be in pointed angles, and if the dog should get mixed up with the angles, take him on the line and assist him to manipulate a few, praise him, and let him try again.

Exercise 55.—The dog follows fresh scent, 30 minutes old, interrupted by two ditches, and gives tongue on finding the assistant. Words of command: *"Follow," "Find."*

The object of this exercise is to force the dog to rely absolutely on his nose, and, when interrupted, to find ways and means by his own efforts to perform his duty.

Method: Practise as in Exercise 53, and for obstacle choose a ditch. The assistant should go up to the ditch in a straight line, jump across, turn immediately to the right, walk alongside the ditch for 50 yards, jump back, and return to within 50 yards of the starting place, and there hide himself. The whole track should not be more than 200 yards. For the second practice the assistant after crossing should turn to the left, but always take care that he never crosses his previous track. For the third practice the assistant, after crossing the second time, should proceed in curves and half-circles to the place where he is going to hide. After the dog has given tongue for about twenty minutes close the exercise, but never forget to reward him after each practice.

Repetition frequently.

Exercise 56.—The dog follows fresh scent, 35 minutes old, the track leading over some boarded fence, and gives tongue on finding the assistant. Words of command: " *Follow*," " *Find*."

The object of this exercise is to teach the dog to follow a scent across high obstacles.

Method: The assistant goes on a straight track, 200 yards long, and on his way climbs across a boarded fence, and at the end of the track lies down and hides himself. The dog must find him and give tongue. For the second practice, the assistant, after crossing the fence, should finish his track in a half circle and close to the fence. For the third practice the assistant should make a half circle on the other side of the fence, but re-cross it and then hide. Let the dog give tongue about ten minutes.

Repetition frequently.

Exercise 57.—The dog follows a fresh scent, 10 to 15 minutes old, across some public and much frequented street, and gives tongue on finding the assistant. Words of command: " *Follow*," " *Find*."

The object of this exercise is to bring the dog to such a pitch of perfection in nosework that he can trace a given scent across others, and across similar ones.

Method: Arrange for the assistant to cross some well-frequented street, then to return to it in a half circle and continue along the street in a zig-zag line for a short distance, and then leaving it again jump across some channel or ditch, then proceed in a winding line to the hiding place. Every track should be 200 yards long, and at the end the assistant has always to lie on the ground, well hidden. The dog gives tongue for about ten minutes.

Repetition frequently.

Exercise 58.—The dog follows a fresh scent, 10 to 20 minutes old, across a much-frequented place, and along streets ending in some isolated dwelling. Words of command: " *Follow*," " *Find*."

The object of this exercise is to make nosework second nature to the dog.

Method: The assistant goes as far as possible in a straight line across much-frequented streets, and then enters some isolated house, leaving the door open. After ten minutes the dog starts. For the second practice the assistant leaves the entrance door open, but enters a room and closes the door. On your arrival you praise the dog and open the door, and inside the room the dog has to give tongue on discovering the assistant.

For the third practice the assistant shuts the entrance door and goes upstairs, closing the doors behind him. On your arrival you open one door after another, and let the dog give tongue at each, and also at the assistant when discovered. Be lavish with your praise, and reward the dog.

Repetition frequently.

Exercise 59.—The dog follows fresh scent, 20 to 40 minutes old, about 200 yards long, and gives tongue on discovering the assistant up a tree. Words of command: " *Follow*," " *Find*."

The object of this exercise is to teach the dog to look for the lost scent in all possible directions, as criminals frequently hide in trees.

Method: Practise as in No. 58, but follow the dog quickly so that you are at hand when the dog loses the scent. The assistant should remain quiet as you approach the tree where he is hidden, and you then show the dog the scent very carefully, and follow it up to the trunk of the tree, and once there the dog will notice the scent on the trunk, and look upwards, and just at this moment order " Speak," and as soon as the dog gives tongue, the assistant should make some movement to disclose his presence. For the second practice, let the scent be 30 minutes old, and 40 minutes for the third one.

One repetition.

Exercise 60.—The dog follows an older scent after having been put on it. Word of command: " *Quietly* " (to quieten the dog, and restrain him from too great haste and eagerness).

The object of this exercise is to teach the dog to follow old scents though they may be crossed with fresher ones.

N.B.—Be very calm and patient when going through this exercise, and don't start when you are tired, excited or in an ill-humour. Practise most minutely, and see that the dog does the same, otherwise there will be no chance to teach him this most difficult accomplishment.

Method: Arrange with the assistant for him to deposit at a given time and place one of his personal objects, then to move on in a straight line for about 100 yards, and there to hide himself. Exactly an hour afterwards you appear on the scene with your dog, which should be wearing a collar, fairly broad, not too tight round the neck, and fastened like any ordinary one (*i.e.*, not a self-acting training collar), and with the 20 yards line attached. The dog begins by finding and fetching the assistant's dropped object, at which you make him smell and sniff well, after which take the dog to the beginning of the footprints made by the assistant. Place yourself over the dog, and with the utmost care point to the footprints, seeing that the dog's nose nearly touches them, and then order, " Follow," " Quietly," " Find." If the dog holds his head very low, praise him. Place the line between the dog's front and hind legs, thus he will be forced to work with his head low down, but as soon as he works well, and has acquired the right position, no longer have him fastened to the line in that position, but repeat it if the dog gets careless or over-anxious. Now let the dog " Follow," but every two yards or steps you stop, and standing over the dog, you again point most carefully to the footprints or let the dog show them to you, and if he is successful be lavish with your praise, and show your great delight. You yourself must keep calm, and show not the slightest trace of haste or impatience; on the contrary, your looks, your voice, your whole bearing must produce a calming effect on the dog. Thus you work carefully along, step by step, and watching closely that the dog's nose never quits the scent either to right or left. To get to the end of the 100 yards where the assistant is hiding should take at least half an hour. The assistant lies quietly in his hiding place and only gets up after the dog has found him; and when he gets up, the dog, loosed from the line, has to give tongue at him at a few yards' distance for about ten minutes.

After this, put the dog on the line, praise and reward him, and take him for a walk, and no further nosework during that day.

On the second day the assistant goes 200 yards and hides in some empty barn or outhouse. You proceed as on the previous day for about 50 yards, and then stop every ten yards, step over the dog, and let him show you the scent, and if he pulls on the line, order, but always in a persuasive tone, " Quietly," " Quietly." If the dog should quit the scent, or follow on one side of it, call out in a voice of displeasure, " Shame ! " and quit the scent, return in a half circle to the starting point and begin afresh. Exact the most perfect performance from the dog from the first day, because it is the only way to get the dog to follow old scents later on, and scents moreover weakened and made diffi-cult to follow by all kinds of circumstances or accidents. At last, when you have arrived in front of the empty building, let the dog give tongue in front of the closed door, open the door, and again let him give tongue at the assistant, after having found him. Now put the dog on the line, praise him, and take the customary walk. On the third day let the scent be 1½ hours old, 500 yards long, and the assistant to hide in some lonely house with the door closed. You yourself, as well as the dog, have not the faintest idea of the whereabouts of the assistant, except that you know the exact starting point. Every 30 yards or so let the dog show you the scent, and when doing so always stand over him. If the dog should get restless, let him show the scent more often, and never mind if it takes you an hour and a half, or two hours, to work the scent; be very patient, and avoid all hasty or careless work. Let the dog give tongue at the closed door, then open the door, and freed from the line the dog must find the assistant, whether in room, cellar or attic, and must give tongue on finding him. Lastly, put the dog on the line, praise and reward him, and let him have his desired walk. On the fourth day the assistant again makes a track of 500 yards, and hides in a well-stocked barn, dropping on the way a few of his personal objects. You begin work with the dog 1½ hours afterwards. Go through the exercise most carefully, and see that the dog finds and fetches the dropped objects, and praise him each time, and each time also let him re-take the scent, showing it to you, and in your turn show your pleasure and approval when he does it well. The assistant remains in hiding beneath the straw, you order the dog to give tongue in front of the straw, which you then personally clear away, until the assistant is totally revealed, when the dog should give tongue again. After this put the dog on the line, praise and reward him, and take him for the usual walk.

NOTE.—*This work cannot be done in reality as quickly as described : again and again one has to re-start, for every new move has to be well impressed on the dog's mind before you can proceed to the next one. The assistant must be changed frequently, and occasionally females must be substituted. And last, but not least, by these exercises you yourself should learn to recognise footprints easily, and as easily to follow them.*

Exercise 61.—The dog, on the line, follows old scent across much-frequented streets. Words of command: " *Follow*," " *Quietly*," " *Find.*"

The object of this exercise is to make the dog perfect in nosework, and to teach the trainer to become more expert in the handling of a Police dog.

Method: About 7 a.m. let the assistant start a 500 yards long track in the following manner. From the starting point he goes towards the much-frequented street, and follows it about 100 yards in a straight line and leaves it, if possible, by jumping across some ditch, either to the right or left, then in a winding line seeks his hiding-place, which may be a house, barn, shed or tree, or he may lie flat upon a wall, but you must not know his hiding-place. On the road itself he should drop a few personal objects and leave some sign or mark where he left the road and jumped the ditch. Work the dog calmly and with much deliberation, let him fetch all the dropped objects in proper and orthodox fashion, and every 30 yards let him show you the scent with his nose, whilst you are standing over him, and do this particularly on the road. As soon as the dog gets mixed or shows signs of restlessness by not keeping a straight course, or by flagging, return in a half-circle, and start the roadwork afresh. Should the dog be unable to find the scent on the road, order " Follow," and point towards the place where the assistant left the road, where he will discover it very soon. However, if the dog should still fail, get close to the place in a half-circle, and help the dog, repeating until he finds it. Impress upon your own mind the form of the assistant's footprint; a missing nail, or one standing out or driven in deeper than the rest, are good identification signs, as is also a patched sole, or something specially attracting attention in the width or length of the boot, or in the manner of putting it down, etc., etc. All this you must learn to perfection, so that you are able to help the dog, and if need be rectify his mistakes. Hence let the dog show you the footprints where the ground is soft, and you can easily distinguish them. If the dog finds the assistant, free him from the line and let him give tongue for about ten minutes, then fasten him again, praise and reward him, and let him have the usual walk. On the second day make the track 1,000 yards long, and the assistant may go across several roads, jump or go along watercourses, proceeding in winding lines and sharp angles, and dropping divers objects on his track, but in prearranged order, thus enabling you to control the work with accuracy. On the third day let the track again be 1,000 yards, and two hours old, and practise as before, always taking care that the dog works on the track, and not off-side. On the fourth day repeat the same exercise, but let the scent be two and a half hours old. On the fifth day repeat as before, but with the scent three hours old. Never omit to let the dog show you the scent every 30 yards, whilst you are standing over him, and be calm, and take your time. *Only the dog who has learned his lesson step by step, with the utmost care and whose trainer never lost patience, can be of any certain success in cases of crime.*

Exercise 62.—The dog follows an escaped criminal after taking the scent inside the prisoner's cell. Words of command: " *Follow,*" " *Quietly,*" " *Find.*"

The object of this exercise is to train the dog to pick up the scent in the empty cell, and follow the escaped individual.

Method: During this exercise frequently change your assistant. The assistant must always leave the building by a different way than by which he entered, and must never cross his own track. He should also have a special mark on his heel or sole, a round or square nail, as the case may be, in order that you can easily recognise the footprint. Let the assistant enter the cell and sit or lie on the bed for about a quarter of an hour, leave nothing in the cell, and then go out, proceed only 100 yards and get into hiding. An hour after you enter the cell with the dog, but don't cross the assistant's track outside the door. Close the door behind you, let the dog loose, and make him sniff all over, and take full advantage of the prisoner's (assistant's) left scent.   After about five minutes put the dog on the line, open the door, and order " Follow," " Quietly." Follow the dog slowly, and as soon as you come to a place where you can possibly recognise the assistant's footprint let the dog show it, and proceed like this, looking at the footprint every 25 yards. After you have found the assistant, take the dog off the line, let him give tongue for about 10 minutes, fasten him again, praise and reward him, and take him for his walk.   On the second day select a room in the Police Station with two doors.   The assistant enters through one, and later on you make your entrance through the other.   The assistant should lie on the floor for a quarter of an hour and then leave by the window, and after proceeding 500 yard hide himself.   You practise as above, and after the dog has sniffed about for five minutes you take him to the window and order " Follow."   Work slowly and let him show you the footprints as soon as possible, and every 30 yards after, and then proceeding as on the first day.   On the third day the assistant enters the room through the door you previously used, and you enter with the dog through the other door.   The assistant leaves the room by the same door he entered, climbs through a window into another room, and, leaving by the door, goes a track of 1,000 yards and hides.   Let the dog sniff well about, and when leaving the first room order " Follow," but before entering by the window into the second room, let the dog show you the footprint, and standing over him, always make sure of the right footprint before proceeding further.   Work the scent carefully, slowly and patiently, and finish up as above.   On the fourth day let the track be 1,500 yards, and start work on the scent when it is three hours old.

Exercise 63.—The dog seeks for stolen property hidden away inside a house, etc.   Words of command: " *Lost*," " *Fetch*."

The object of this exercise is to teach the dog to find stolen property hidden by the thief, and this by aid of the scent from some object left behind by the thief.

Method: The assistant places one of his well-used gloves on the floor of the room, and three other personal objects he hides inside the room, but in such a way that it is not over difficult to find them, say, below a bed, behind a wardrobe, etc., and, of course, you know what the objects are.   The assistant clears out, and after an hour you enter with the dog.   Let the dog loose, and, pointing to the floor, order " Lost," " Fetch."   After the dog has fetched the glove, praise him and order again, " Lost," " Fetch," repeating this until he has brought all the objects, always encouraging him meanwhile.   Lastly, put him on the line, give him some special praise, reward him, and be off for his walk. On the second day the assistant leaves his glove in the passage, the next object on the top of the stairs, and the rest under other objects, in order that you have to assist to get them from underneath.   You start two hours afterwards, and as soon as the dog begins to whine, give tongue, or scratch when he has found the hidden object and cannot get at it, help him at once to get it.   Always let him bring them, " sit " and " drop " them, and let him again sniff at them, and after praising him well, send him for the next by ordering " Lost," " Fetch."   Lastly, finish the exercise as on the first day.   On the third day the assistant leaves the glove in the passage, and hides the rest of the objects in more difficult places, but always within reach of the dog.   You yourself do not know how or where they are hidden, but you know the objects and their number. After three hours you start work with the dog, and after he has fetched the glove in the passage, proceed as above, and finish in the same manner. Practise frequently later on.

Exercise 64.—The dog learns not to be gun-shy.

The object of this exercise is to get the dog not to be frightened at the firing of a shot, and also to attack the one who shoots, unless it be his trainer, or an officer in uniform.

Method: Your assistant stands 100 yards distant from you with revolver or gun and blank cartridges. Tell him to fire whenever you lift up your hand. Order the dog to " sit," but with his back towards the assistant, order " Stop," watch the dog and signal to the assistant. If the dog stops, let the assistant approach 25 yards nearer and fire again —and another 25 yards if the dog still remains sitting. If the dog keeps on sitting, order " Come," and make a large circle round the assistant, who must then go on firing at short intervals; lessen the circle down to 20 yards, watch your dog, and speak to him precisely at the moment the assistant shoots, then finish for the day.

On the second day the assistant holds the line of the sitting dog, standing behind him, and you, 75 yards in front, start firing your revolver in the air. The assistant then approaches you slowly with the dog, and when within 20 yards he stops short, you turn round and give the pre-arranged signal with your left hand for the assistant to slip the dog, at the same time fire again, and then praise and reward the quickly-approaching dog, and have your walk.

Repeat the second part of the exercise more or less frequently. If the dog is gun-shy at 100 yards, then don't let the assistant approach, but let him recede 25 yards, and then fire again. Be kind to the dog, speak nicely to him, and pat him all the time. Walk round the assistant in a large circle; meanwhile he fires on and off, and always speak kindly to the dog just at the moment the assistant is going to fire. Repeat this until the dog is cured. Afterwards take the dog to shooting range, but approach from behind, so that the sound of the firing increases by degrees.

Exercise 65.—The dog is trained to attack his quarry. Word of command: *"Fight."*

NOTE.—*This exercise must not be practised until the dog is well trained, perfectly in hand, and reliable under all conditions ; for the Police dog must not turn out a wild, savage brute, but an assistant, and a helpful weapon in his master's hand.*

The object of this exercise is to train the dog not only as heretofore, simply to assist his master, but to assist and defend him with all his powers. The dog will learn fearlessly to seize and pull down any aggressor, whether his master or he himself be attacked, and to do it with the least possible bodily damage, ceasing at once when the enemy gives in.

First Degree : The dog gives tongue at the sight of the assistant with the dummy inside the training room, and gets hold of the latter's arm.

Method: The assistant with the dummy stands behind the boarding inside the training room. You enter with the dog on the line, and take a few turns, when suddenly the assistant starts knocking loudly at the boarding, and at the same time lifting the dummy's head above the boarding. You stop short in your walk and quickly face the boarding, drawing the dog's attention to the dummy's head. If the dog gives tongue on his own account, praise him, if not order " Speak," and let him give plenty of tongue. After a few minutes the assistant shows the dummy's arm at the side of the boarding, and through this he holds a stick with which he makes as though to strike at the dog, but whenever the dog advances, pulls back the stick, arm and head of the dummy, thus, giving the dog the impression that his enemy is in fear and frightened of him. After the first hit at the dog order " Fight," and encourage him well. For the beginning do not approach too near, and always let the dog be under the impression that the dummy is hitting at him. After a while, and when the dog shows no fear, step a yard nearer and always encourage him by ordering " Fight." Now let the dog loose, order " Fight," and if the dog does not grip the dummy's arm at once let the assistant give him a slight rap with the stick, which, with your encouragement by ordering " Fight," will make him attack. As soon as the dog seizes the dummy's arm or hand, the assistant should keep still, and you must call the dog off. The dog must be taught to obey at once, and under no consideration must he start shaking. Praise the dog and take a few turns round the room without him being on the line. After a while the dummy starts again, you stop, and if need be, order " Speak," then " Fight," and repeat as above, finishing after half an hour's practice. After the dog is proficient, the assistant then hits at him personally, but must have on a suit and gloves well padded, and by degrees removes his whole body from behind the boarding. Repeat this exercise daily until the dog, on the least whisper of " Fight," takes hold of the dummy's arm. He must only grip once, and stick to it until the assistant is quiet, when he must be immediately called off, and must always obey most promptly.

Second Degree : The dog throws down and guards the runaway criminal.

Method : The assistant, in his thick protection suit, stands behind the boarding inside the training room. With the dog on line you enter the room and take a few turns. When you are at the other end of the room the assistant taps at the boarding and comes out from behind it, at which you stop and let the dog give tongue. The assistant approaches, hits at you, and starts shouting and abusing you. Slip the dog, which must not, however, attack without the order, and now the assistant slightly hits you, and then turns and runs for all he is worth. Order " Fight," and follow the assistant, meanwhile encouraging the dog to jump on to the running assistant's back. As soon as the dog jumps, the assistant throws himself down on to his face and keeps very still. Praise the dog, and order " Drop." Then let the dog lie down across, and about two yards in front of the assistant and put the line down as well. Step behind the dog and keep your eyes on him. Now let the assistant hit at the dog with his stick, when you quickly order " Fight," and step nearer. As soon as the dog grips, the assistant lies still, and you order " Drop " or whistle the dog off. Repeat a few times, then with the dog leave the room. After some time, and the assistant again being hidden, enter once more with the dog and repeat as before. Practise in this way until the dog, when ordered " Fight," with one jump throws the man, and immediately lies down, but attacks him again when he tries to rise, or hits at him. It must become second nature to the dog to know that he should never attack quietly-standing or still-lying people.

Third Degree : The dog watches his quarry and prevents his flight during the absence of his master.

Method: After the dog has thrown the assistant, and is lying down guarding him inside the training room, you leave the room and watch the dog through the spy-hole in the door. As soon as the assistant endeavours to get up you order " Fight," but later on leave the dog without orders. As soon as the dog grips the moving assistant he must always lie still at once, otherwise the dog will grow too excited and begin to bite and tear the protection clothes. The dog has to be trained for the actual event, when to bite is really necessary. If the dog should show fear, and allow the assistant to get up, intervene at once and assist the dog encouragingly; if, on the other hand, no fear is shown, enter the room after some time and praise the dog well. Watch carefully that the dog never touches the still-lying assistant, and that he always lies two or three yards from the assistant, who should be crosswise in front of the dog.

Fourth Degree : The dog attacks and throws in the open a criminal who assaulted either him or his master, and assists to take him to the lock-up.

Method: Go with your trained dog into the open country, where the assistant, in his protection suit, meets you. The dog is free. The assistant starts abusing you, and shakes his stick at you. Now stop with the dog; the assistant approaches, shouting and swinging his stick, and gives the dog a rap. At once you order " Fight," but directly the dog seizes the assistant's arm or stick he must give in and stand still, and you call or whistle the dog off. After the dog has returned to his place, the assistant hits at you and starts running away; let him run a few yards, then order " Fight "; you follow the dog quickly, and when he has jumped on the assistant's back he should subsequently take the " on guard " position when the assistant has thrown himself down on his face and remains motionless. Leave the dog with the assistant and go some distance away, and watch him. If the dog does not allow the assistant to move, leave him alone, otherwise order " Fight." After a few minutes approach, call or whistle off the dog, handcuff the assistant and march towards the lock-up. After you have gone 50 or 60 yards the assistant suddenly stops and makes an attack on you. Take hold of the assistant's neck from the back, order " Fight," at the same time motioning the dog to jump right on to the back of the assistant, who at once throws himself face downward and keeps quiet. Order the dog " Rest," and go away, but watch the dog and see that he does not allow the assistant to move at all. After some minutes approach, call or whistle the dog off, praise him, and continue your march prisonwards. When the dog has become fairly well trained, retire out of sight altogether, but secretly creep up and watch, and let the dog know that you are near by ordering him to do his duty, should he neglect it. Repeat until the dog is proficient and reliable.

Fifth Degree : The dog attacks the running criminal—who shoots—and sticks to him until his master arrives.

Method: Start your practice as usual, when having your dog on the line, the assistant strikes you and runs off. Slip the dog, but slowly, so as to give the assistant a start of about 20 to 25 yards, and order " Fight." The assistant stops, turns round, and fires the revolver into the air, when you at once repeat " Fight," then see that the dog attacks the assistant from behind in the usual way, after which he drops, and you order " Rest." Go a little distance away and proceed as above, but the assistant must not shoot during your absence, and must always lie quiet after the first bite. After this, practise with two assistants, who are walking side by side, you following with the dog. One of the two runs away, you seize the remaining assistant, and order " Fight," pointing to the one running away. Watch that the dog " rests " if the fugitive comes to a standstill and remains motionless, or if the dog throws him down, does his duty to perfection.

Sixth Degree : The dog follows the scent of the criminal, gives tongue on finding him, and attacks him, after the criminal has fired a shot.

Method: The assistant leaves some personal object at a pre-arranged spot, proceeds some 100 yards further away, and hides. After about ten minutes, you turn up where the object lies. Let the dog " fetch " the object in the proper manner, then let him sniff well at it, and order " Follow." The assistant keeps still, and dog only gives tongue when he has found him. You follow leisurely, and when you are within ten yards of the hiding place the assistant should shoot and start running away. The dog, without any order, must straightaway attack him; if he does not, you order " Fight," which, however, will not be needed if you have gone through the practices thoroughly. You must take care that the assistant never hits at the dog, or shoots until you have come near, and that the dog does not attack when the assistant stands or lies quietly, but at the most gives tongue.

Seventh Degree : The dog attacks the assistant, who strikes at him in the dark.

Method: At a pre-arranged spot, and in the dark, you meet your assistant, who hits your dog, which is about ten yards in front of him, and then runs away. At once order " Fight." Repeat until the dog, without word of command, follows, attacks, and does as practised above.

Eighth Degree : The dog is attacked inside the house and he defends himself.

Method: The assistant stands inside the house, of course in his suit; you open the door, and he hits the dog at once. You order " Fight," etc., etc. Go through similar practices to these; the 7th and 8th will teach the dog to be careful and take precautions.

Exercise 66.—Looking for lost or hidden people, or objects. Word of command: " *Search.*"

The object of this exercise is to teach the dog to examine carefully, and seek systematically, in a zig-zag line, thickets, outhouses, sheds, or ditches, etc., and to fetch things that he finds, or, if they are too heavy for him, to give tongue until his master arrives.

NOTE.—As it is of the utmost importance that the Police dog should not only find lost objects, but also should be able to discover hidden people, lost people, or people who have met with an accident, and as no dog has a natural gift to do this in a practical and systematic manner, the trainer has to go through the four following degrees with great painstaking and the utmost thoroughness.

First Degree : Go early in the morning to a quiet retired spot, but where the ground is open, and where no disturbing elements of any kind are likely to be met with. Practise with the dog in a zig-zag line as shown in Fig. 1. Having the dog on the line, begin at A, pointing with your right hand towards B on the right, and order " Search." Let the dog be about three yards in front. At point B you stop and point with your left hand towards point C on the left, and thus proceed from point to point, but on the last but one turn throw some personal object of yours, unknown and unseen by the dog, in such a position that

he is bound to find it. After the next and last turn, let him fetch and
deliver it in the proper manner, then praise him and stop the exercise.
On the second day practise on the same ground, but order " Search "
once only at the beginning, afterwards alone indicating the direction for

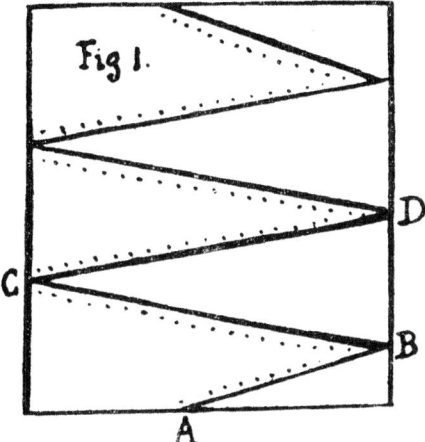

seeking by movements of the right or left hand respectively. After the
third day choose places for practice well covered with shrubs and

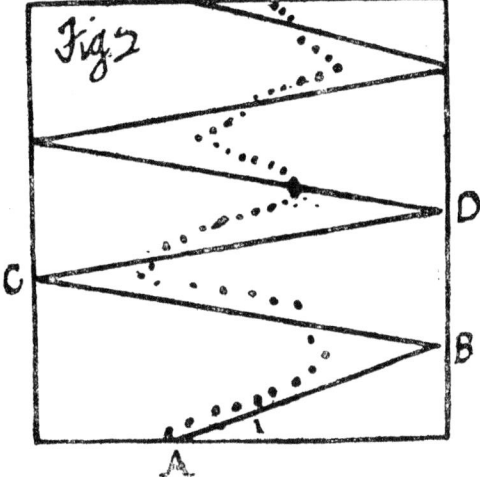

bushes. On the seventh day let the dog find the assistant hidden in
some bush or ditch, or behind a wall, the dog giving tongue on finding
him. On the eighth day let the dog find a box in the centre, and give
tongue on finding it, and finally the assistant at the end of the track,
when he gives tongue again. On the ninth day let the dog find one
assistant earlier, and at the finish another one, and at both he must give

tongue. On the tenth day he finds the first assistant about in the centre of the exercise ground motionless with face downward, and the dog has to give tongue, and at the second one he must give tongue on finding him at the finish hiding in some bush.

Second Degree : Observe Fig. 2; the lines represent the way the dog has to go, and the dotted track the way you must walk. Start as on the first day, but let the dog loose, point with right hand and order " Search " and follow, and as soon as he has reached point B you turn and point with the left hand to point C without further ordering; thus continue, always making your turns shorter than those the dog has to take. Never call or whistle; the dog must learn to watch you. During the first ten days the dog only finds something at the finish; afterwards he finds the box and the assistants as above. Practise calmly, and go with the dog now and then, should he not make his turns and angles properly. Fifteen to twenty exercises are needed at least to get him to perfection.

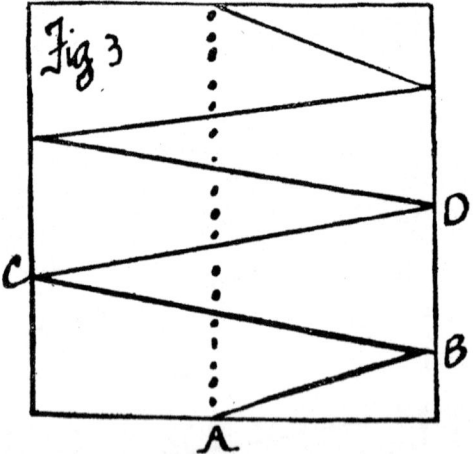

Third Degree : Observe Fig. 3. You shorten your way until you walk in a straight line, but never hurry, and see that the dog works correctly. At the beginning of the turnings you must give the signal with the right or left hand respectively until the dog has learned and understood what to do on hearing the command " Search."

Fourth Degree : Practise now in twilight, afterwards in full moonlight, then in the dark, and lastly during dark and stormy nights. Let the assistant hide himself in some place, of which you know the whereabouts, but not the exact spot. The assistant must not under any consideration be of any help to the dog, which must find him unaided, and straight away give tongue. Afterwards let the assistant put on his protection clothes and hide in some haystack or strawrick, then make the dog search the ground thoroughly and arrange it so that the dog must find him in the long run. Finally, the assistant, being discovered by the dog and you having come up on the dog's call, attacks you. Always arrange the searching of the place according to the topographical surroundings, and be always patient when the dog makes a mistake, and never fail to show your satisfaction when he is doing well. Finally, bear well in mind that, when a mistake does occur, the fault is yours, and not the dog's.

Exercise 67.—Waterwork.

NOTE.—The dog must not be forced to enter water, and under no consideration must he be thrown in. Many dogs, like human beings, have a natural aversion for, or fear of, water. The dog has to enter the water first, because he has learned to obey, and secondly you have to try and make him enjoy entering it. The waterwork has to begin when the water is warm, thus it will do the dog good and he will enjoy it without fear of catching cold. In every case the dog has to be perfect in " fetching " on land before this exercise can be begun with any hope of success. The dog has first to become accustomed to water, then has to exercise his swimming powers, and finally, after he has learned there is no danger for him in the wet element, you may start with the waterwork proper. The object of this exercise is to teach the Police dog to fetch objects out of the water, to bring to land corpses and dead animals, and to assist drowning people in saving their lives, but he must not be trained for any tricks or play purposes. The dog must remain under the impression that it is a serious business, and not play.

First Degree : Take the dog on the short line to some shallow stream and walk hither and thither. The water must be very shallow. Leave the water, order " Sit," praise him, then have another walk in the shallow water. First walk close to the bank with your left foot nearly touching it, and afterwards with the bank to your right; watch carefully that the water is not too deep, thus hindering the dog in walking. Arrange that suddenly the dog is forced to swim by your side, but do not let him swim more than a yard or two. Come out of the water, order " Sit," and praise him lavishly. Practise again; be kind and speak encouragingly to him, praise him, and never show temper or impatience.

On the third day the assistant takes the dog on the opposite bank. Arrange that the dog first has to enter shallow water before he has to swim, see also that there is no bridge or shallow passage across in proximity. Call for the dog to come across, or whistle, and then walk away. The assistant slips him, and after the dog has reached you order " Sit," and let him well understand that you are pleased with his performance.

Second Degree : The dog fetches the wooden block out of shallow water.

Method: Have a special block for this purpose, rather thin in the centre, then the dog can grip it better. Let the dog " fetch " the block at least ten times on land before you put him on the line, then throw the block a few yards in the shallow water and order " Fetch." Watch that the dog does not put down the block when leaving the water to shake himself, but that he comes up to you and at once " sits " down. Wait a little while until you order " Drop," and take the block from him. If the dog tries to " drop " the block after leaving the water call sharply " Shame," and give him a short, sharp pull with the line, then throw the block further in, and enter the water along with the dog, ordering " Fetch." Come out with him and walk a little distance from the water before ordering " Sit," and " Drop." After the dog does the preliminary work well, throw the block in water where it swims, but where the dog has still to wade to fetch it. Be patient and show delight at good and quick work, and thus the dog will get a liking and finally a passion for this kind of work. Repetition, five times, half an hour each time.

Third Degree : The dog fetches the block out of deep and running water.

Method: Let the dog fetch the block a few times out of shallow water, and free from the line, then enter the water with the dog on the line; keep the bank to your right-hand side, and walk with the stream. Throw the block in such a position that the dog can only reach it by a short swim, and order " Fetch." Go with the dog, and as soon as he has caught hold of the block leave the water, order " Sit," praise him, and then " Drop." When re-entering the water let the dog, having caught hold of the block, swim a little by your side. Don't practise too long in one day.

On the second day, try if the dog will " fetch " the block and come out of the water with you without being on the line; if not, keep him on the line until he has lost all fear. Even if you let him loose from the line, still enter the water with him for some time, then later on throw from the river bank and order " Fetch," and always throw it further in. Never choose a bank where the dog cannot get out easily. Don't practise too long on one day, and only on warm days; thus the dog feels a natural inclination to go in. Eight or ten repetitions.

Fourth Degree : The dog fetches the dummy. Words of command: " *Help*," " *Fetch*."

Method: Take a wooden dummy dressed as a man, and now and then as a woman, put it in shallow water a few yards from the bank. Having the dog on the line, you turn up, and, seeing it, you must point it out to the dog, and ordering " Help," " Fetch," you enter the water with him. Get him to grip at the upper arm and nowhere else, thus laying the foundation to save life without hurting the drowning person and with the least possible exertion. As soon as the dog has caught hold, assist him to get the dummy to the bank, then praise and reward him. Never practise more than two or three times in succession. The main point in this exercise is not for the dog to drag the dummy a long distance, but for him to take hold of it properly. Now get an assistant to put the dummy in deep water, and by means of some packthread hold it in position and from floating away. You turn up with the dog, and seeing the dummy in the water, you point it out to the dog and show anxiety. Order " Help," " Fetch," and quickly enter the water with the dog. Watch that the dog takes hold properly, help him to get the dummy to land, then praise him, and don't forget a reward. Practise only twice in a day; and after the dog understands that he has to take hold of the dummy in the one way only, let him fetch it out of the water by himself, and from longer distances.   Ten repetitions.

Fifth Degree : The dog saves a person. Words of command: " *Help*," " *Fetch*."

Take an assistant, a good swimmer, with light clothes, but with the upper arms wrapped in towels, and with swimming belt, and let him lie in deep water. When you arrive on the scene you pretend some excitement and order "Help," " Fetch," pointing out the assistant to the dog. Enter the water with the dog, and see that he takes hold in the correct way, and then help him to get the assistant to land. After that the assistant jumps into the water from the bank, or a boat, and the dog, receiving orders " Help," " Fetch," goes to the rescue by himself, but you must always help the dog when coming close to the bank. Order him to " Sit," and praise and reward him after each exercise. Practise twice only in one day, in order that the dog's strength may not be over-taxed. Repetition: Whenever climatic conditions permit.

Exercise 68.—Working of old and half-dissolved scents.

Old scents can only be traced by the dog in little-frequented roads and places, and whoever expects a dog to do this in busy streets in towns and cities, or on asphalt and stone pavements, shows a very lamentable ignorance of the subject.

Method: Let the assistant pursue a course across some fields and meadows, etc., in such a way that later he returns to the finishing point without crossing or touching his own track. Let the scent be twelve to eighteen hours old, and later on a day and a half, that is when the ground is good and favourable. When you start the following day the assistant must be in his place, as it is most important that the exercise is gone through from start to finish. Let the dog show you the track every 30 yards or so; work slowly and patiently, and if the dog loses the scent, act as on former occasions. Of course, on finding the assistant he must give tongue as usual.

Exercise 69.—The dog discovers amongst divers persons the right man.
Words of command: " *Follow*," " *Find*."

The object of this exercise is to teach the dog to pick out amongst a number of people by the aid of his scent the one person to whom an object left behind belongs.

Method: Place in a room three or four, and later more persons, having previously taken from one of them some personal object, and let the dog sniff well at it, then order " Follow," " Find." Watch that the dog gives tongue as soon as he has discovered the right person. Praise and reward him well. Repetition: Whenever you have an opportunity.

Exercise 70.—The dog takes the scent in some place and seeks and finds amongst different people's garments one whose owner's scent was left in the place referred to.

The object of this exercise is to teach the dog by means of his scenting power to select from wearing apparel of divers persons that belonging to the wearer, who left absolutely nothing in a given place except his scent.

Method: Place some wearing apparel of your assistant's and of two other persons in separate boxes, and place the three boxes in the passage of the house. Let your assistant enter a room through the window, and let it be a room in which no one has been for some days; let him lie on the floor for a quarter of an hour, then leave the room through the window again. Take the dog into the room, order " Follow " and let him sniff well for about five minutes, then open the door and follow him to the boxes close by. Let the boxes be open with the lid facing towards the front. As soon as the dog shows that he has recognised the apparel of the same scent and does not give tongue, order him to do so. Repetition: First few successive days, and afterwards whenever occasion and circumstances are convenient.

N.B.—In all these exercises bear in mind the general instructions given at the beginning of Part 2, and give the words of command in a calm, gentle voice, for habitual harshness is sure to make the dog frightened or sulky, when he cannot do good work. Finally, this is a point upon which too great stress cannot be laid. A want of patience and a habit of shouting at and threatening the dog are the two greatest faults that I have observed in the trainer, who will never find his efforts crowned with success until his own impatience has been overcome and his own temper is absolutely under control. Then, and not until then, can we hope to have a body of Police dogs which will be a credit to the Constabulary, a menace to the evil-doer, and a source of praise and admiration to the whole law-abiding portion of the community.

ON THE TRAIL WITH A POLICE DOG

Some Adventures from Real Life

MISSING FROM HOME

The striking demonstration of a bloodhound's scenting power in a recent murder case recalls to the writer other instances wherein this delicate sense of smell solved mysteries of divers kinds. The one about to be related did not concern crime, but was one of those " missing from home " cases now much more common than in earlier days. To spare the feelings of relatives the story was hushed up as much as possible at the time, but as none are alive to-day it may be told in detail.

One October morning, in the early part of the present century, as the clock in the market place of the little north country town of S—— was striking eight, the telephone bell in the nearby Police Station tinkled shrilly. The officer in charge, unhooking the receiver, was told the housekeeper at the Hall was speaking. She stated her master had left home shortly before dinner time the previous evening wearing his dinner jacket, but without hat or overcoat. He had gone ostensibly to see his gamekeeper, but the gamekeeper, now at the Hall, had never seen or heard anything of him.

The missing gentleman was the leading man in the district, prominent on the local Bench, chairman of the Guardians and District Council. A wealthy bachelor of sporting tastes, his leisure hours were mostly passed in shooting and fishing, though a decline in his keenness for sport had been observed recently, and much of his time had lately been passed in the Hall garden, which he paced absorbed in meditation.

Needless to say, with this news the Police became busy. Telephones and telegrams were employed, and all likely persons interviewed, but the hours sped away without bringing any clue. A council of war was held, and it was determined to make a trial of " Nightshade," a bloodhound, who just previously had tracked down a notorious sheep stealer. When this decision was made nearly nine hours had elapsed, and it was in the fading light of the dying day that the trainer and his hound came on the scene.

The first question to settle was the one of scent, and here it must be remembered that the bloodhound has the ability to remember any particular scent. One of the missing man's gloves—that article of attire where scent lingers longest—was procured and given to " Nightshade " to smell; and with the trainer's finger pointed to the ground, he was ordered " Follow " " find." For a while the hound snuffled around the garden quite mute, with tail and ears indicating his uncertainty, until he reached a wicket gate in one corner. There, for a moment, he stood tense and motionless, then raising his head sounded that long, loud, deep and melodious bay which is a sure signal of finding the scent. Following this, he leaped the gate into a plantation, through which he wound his way, emerging into a field, crossed it, shaped a course along the hedge side, and descended into an obscure lane, once a road for pack horses, now grass grown and derelict.

So far, there had been no hesitation since the hound left the Hall garden, but now the pace became slower and more uncertain. Once, quite at a loss, " Nightshade " retraced his steps, yet pacified and encouraged by his trainer, he continued his efforts. Shortly again rang out that bell-like bay, and, step by step onward the hound marked his way. Now the lane was left, the trail leading up a bank into a small copse. By this time it was entirely dark, and only the rustling of the shrubs denoted the direction the hound was taking.   By and by this noise ceased and profound silence reigned. The trainer blew his whistle, and was answered by a prolonged baying. Guided by the sound, he left the copse and could dimly discern the figure of " Nightshade " standing on the brink of a desolate stretch of water, known locally as Jack Hole, a favoured haunt of wild duck and other waterfowl. Here the missing man had been wont to shoot, and here, also, it was apparent the trail ended. Came the daylight, came men with grappling irons, and with these the solution of the mystery.

THE SHOPBREAKER

Time : Just after midnight.   *Place :* A small village on the Yorkshire wolds.   The local grocer was sleeping peacefully in his bedroom over the shop when he was awakened by a loud noise from below.   On going downstairs he found a marauder had been at work; the till had been forced open and the cash abstracted; but the thief had flown.   Hurriedly he dressed, then went out into the street in search of the village Constable. He met him patrolling his beat, and together they returned to the shop.

The Policeman at once made a search for footprints, fingerprints, and any other marks likely to be of use in indicating the perpetrator.   Whilst examining a side window where the catch had been slipped, he espied an old cap lying on the ground just below.   This he covered with a box.

When daylight came he returned to the scene with his bloodhound, " Nightshade," in leash.   Taking the box from the cap, and pointing to the latter for the hound to take the scent, and following by an order to find, he awaited developments.

" Nightshade " cast around for a time, then, giving tongue, led his master up the village street and out on to the high road.   No one was astir, and the hound's ringing bay sounding at intervals was the only noise to break the silence.   Scenting conditions were good as the ground was moist and a mild southerly wind prevailed.

After keeping to the highway for nearly a mile, " Nightshade " stopped at a stile, clambered over and followed a footpath through the fields for half a mile or so, which led to a small hamlet.   Here a few early risers were to be seen standing about their cottage doors, but at the sight of the Policeman and " Nightshade " they hastily retreated inside.   The hound took no notice of them as with nose close to the ground he steadily pursued his task.

Leaving the hamlet, the trail was now up an old lane, soon to debouch on to a stackyard.   This contained several complete stacks, and in one corner a smaller pile.   Towards the latter " Nightshade " made his way, stopped beside it and gave utterance to those bell-like notes.   He continued them repeatedly, signifying his quarry to be not far away.   His master, procuring a pitchfork. started to remove the hay, and presently a man was revealed, his countenance petrified with terror. He was very ragged and very dirty; unmistakably a tramp. Shown the cap, he admitted his guilt, said he had heard the hound's bay just when he was preparing to leave the stack where he had stopped for a rest and a sleep, and had concealed himself in the hope of escaping detection.

THE HAUNTED HOUSE

Dunnow Hall was for sale or to be let furnished. The owner of this ancient manor house standing in one of the most picturesque parts of Yorkshire, fallen on evil times, and compelled to relinquish his ancestral home, was said to have left the district. It was whilst the Hall remained untenanted that rumours began to circulate as to uncanny happenings there. A caretaker who had been installed found his nerves so upset by the flashing of lights, direful moans and knockings on the panelled walls that he left in a hurry. It was when these tidings reached the firm of solicitors acting for the new owners that the Police were called in to take a hand.

The Sergeant of Dunnow Section, entrusted with the case, first paid a daylight visit to the Hall alone. There was no sign of any living object there, the most careful examination failing to reveal anything out of the ordinary, but silence, like a heavy pall, brooded over the whole place. After dark another visit was made, this time the Sergeant taking with him the Dunnow Constable and his bloodhound " Nightshade." Before opening the great door the men made an inspection of the front of the house from the lawn. To their surprise a central window was illuminated by an eerie, forlorn looking light, that made it stand out in contrast to the rest. On unlocking the door and going inside they found the light had disappeared, and there was no sign of any of the oil lamps, the only illuminant then at the Hall, having been lit. At a signal from his master, " Nightshade " began to " nose " around, and with lanterns open the Policemen followed in his wake. It was whilst they were upstairs that a muffled hammering was heard below; then a voice carried up to them; then hammering again; but all was heard as through wood. Rushing down, they made for the dining room, from where the noises seemed to be coming. There was nobody there; the hammering had ceased, and the voice was silent. Their attention was now directed to " Nightshade," who, for the first time, was betraying symptoms of uneasiness. Snuffling round the room, panelled from floor to ceiling, he paused by the fireplace, then placing his front feet on the panel above the open hearth, he let out, not his usual deep bay, but a low mournful whine. Puzzled, the men minutely examined the flooring, the fireplace, the wainscot, without finding any clue to account for the hound's behaviour. They remained in the room for a long time, " Nightshade " seeming reluctant to leave, but after he was called from the fireplace and ordered to rest, nothing occurred to break the profound silence. At dawn a very mystified Sergeant and Constable departed for their respective stations.

One day shortly after this, the Sergeant, being on duty in another part of his section, chanced to meet an old man, formerly in service at the Hall. Recounting to him its recent history, he mentioned his visits and the strange behaviour of " Nightshade." Here, the other interrupted him with, " Why, that is where you get into the secret chamber." The old man then explained that by an ingenious device one of the wall's panels could be made to open outwards disclosing an opening which gave access to a small chamber. This, he said, was used in by-gone days as a hiding place for fugitive " Mass priests " and their holy vessels, and he had often shewn it to visitors at the Hall. At the Sergeant's sugges-tion, he agreed to meet him at the Hall that same evening and open the concealed door. When night fell, the two men, together with the blood-hound, entered the house. Once inside the dining room the Sergeant saw his companion turn two of the large wooden buttons with which the fireplace was studded. No sooner had he done this than the innocent looking piece of panelling with the carved shield that covered the wall over the hearth, moved outwards and a great doorway opened, through which showed a black space, large enough to admit a man.

The hound, quivering with excitement, gave tongue when he saw the doorway and then, mute, waited for his master's bidding. Told to " find," he at once sprang through the opening and vanished in the dark-ness. The Sergeant followed. Next came a continued baying. Those sonorous notes proclaimed that " Nightshade " had found his quarry. The Sergeant meanwhile had reached the end of a short passage and by the light of his lantern saw on the left a narrow opening giving access to a small room. Flashing his light around he observed the figure of a man crouching in one corner with " Nightshade " on guard over him. He threw the lantern's rays on the man's face and was astounded to discover it was that of the late owner of the Hall.

Now for the explanation. It seemed this man's action in procuring for the Hall the reputation of being haunted so that it would be difficult to let or sell, was due to a two-fold motive, partly, in revenge for a fancied injustice by the new owners, partly, from an intense dislike of the idea of strangers living in the home of his ancestors. Local tradition has it that the Hall is still haunted, but if the spirits of " Nightshade " and the owner, now both gone to join the great majority, play games of hide and seek about its rooms, the present occupiers are happily insensible of their pranks.

THE MOORLAND POTEEN-MAKER

Before the arrival of the motor age, in the sparsely inhabited moor-lands between Halifax and Oldham dwelt a somewhat wild and lawless people, in many respects resembling their ancestors portrayed for us in the novels of Halliwell Sutcliffe. Cock-fighting, pitch and toss and poteen-making lingered on until quite recent days. It is with the tracking down of probably the last of the poteen-makers that this story deals.

For some time the Excise had reason to believe that quantities of liquor on which no duty had ever been paid were being brought out of this district for sale in Oldham and other towns. All efforts to intercept the liquor or trace the source of supply has so far failed.

While this suspicion was rife it so happened that early one morning the Police Inspector for the district had taken his bloodhound, " Night-shade," up on to the moors for practice in tracking an assistant accom-panying him to act as quarry. It was whilst engaged in this work that one of the men noticed by the side of a small stream what he suspected to be the remains of an illicit still with every sign of recent usage. A nearer inspection disclosed on the the moist ground the footprints of someone who had been there not long ago.

The thought at once occurred—why not try " Nightshade " ? He was therefore brought to the spot and his nose put to the footprints, then the order " Follow," " Find." After one or two efforts the hound picked up the scent, and the moist ground and mild westerly wind helped him in working it out. His trainer followed in the rear with his assistant, and kept a close watch on " Nightshade's " ears and tail, by which his uncertainty could be gauged, so that they could pacify him and encourage him to persevere when necessary.

The conditions for tracking were ideal, ground and air moist, no sign of human life on the moorland footpath, and " Nightshade's " sonorous bark, uttered ever and anon, was, except for the matutinal song of birds, the only sound that broke the silence. It was clear that the scent was comparatively fresh, for the hound ranged high, and did not have to cast back and showed no inclination to potter. Only once did he leave the track and that was to puzzle at a large tuft of bog myrtle, but after he had run round it three or four times, there dubiously crept out an old hare. Satisfied and faithful to his training, " Nightshade " bothered no further about the hare, but with head down and tail going he continued on his way working out the human scent.

After about a mile the trail skirted a hamlet, and then led into the yard of a small moorland farm. Here, in one corner, " Nightshade " stopped, stiffened and gave tongue. After this he made his way to the closed door of the farmhouse, but soon returned to the yard. Meanwhile the Inspector's assistant, investigating in the corner where " Nightshade " stopped, discovered under some rubbish a spiral pipe, essential to the making of poteen and commonly known as the " worm." Nothing else could be found outside, and the next question was how to get into the house, which seemed deserted.

It is the custom of the moor man when he sees strangers approaching his home, to retire into the house, and screened from observation himself, watch their movements through the window. The Inspector, aware of this, took the bull by the horns, and unannounced opened the door and walked straight in. The first thing that he saw was a bowl of " wash," which the farmer in his flurry had forgotten to hide. Confronted with this and the pipe, the farmer, who was found in the parlour, confessed his guilt. He admitted he had brought the pipe and other things from the still that morning, ready for reassembling elsewhere, as it was the practice never to have the still long in one place. He also stated who were his accomplices, as he thought they had betrayed him.

It turned out that the spirit had been conveyed secreted in nosebags tied under carts to the axles, and these farmers' carts laden with young pigs, or, perhaps, crates of poultry, looked innocent enough on their journeys to Oldham or some other place.

HOW AN AIREDALE HELPED HIS MASTER

Most of the inhabitants of Paythorne had retired to rest when the Constable of that quiet little village left his Station for night duty, accompanied by his Airedale terrier, " Bruce." The first hour of this duty he spent within the confines of the village proper and then, as nothing called for his attention there, set off to patrol the outlying parts of his beat and examine the property in his charge.

His first visit was to the Manor House standing away from the high road and secluded within the great walls of the garden. Here, as he had done on numberless other nights, he tried the doors, flashed his lantern light on the windows, finding as he had always done before that all was safe and secure. Satisfied, he turned away from the house, but had not gone far along the drive when " Bruce " growled threateningly—a clear indication that he had got the scent of some other animal or human being, who was not very far away.

" Find," said his master, and into a dense shrubbery at one side of the garden went the dog. Silence for a few moments, then a fierce bark was repeated. Next a man came rushing across the lawn with " Bruce " at his heels. The Constable tried to intercept the man, but failed. However, the dog soon overtook him and brought him to a standstill.

Realising that unless he could rid himself of the dog or his master, capture was imminent, the man drew a pistol from his pocket. The watchful eye of " Bruce " noted his action and trained as he was to attack anyone not in uniform who attempted to shoot, the dog leaped at the man's arm. The pistol went off, but without doing any harm. Before the man could aim and fire again, he received the full impact of the dog's weight and was borne to the ground, the pistol dropping from his hand as he fell. The Constable, who had arrived on the spot as the shot was fired, first possessed himself of the weapon, and then handcuffed the half-dazed man, who was still on the ground.

The prisoner made no further resistance, but walked quietly to the lock-up with the dog on one side and the Constable on the other. Here he was searched and a set of housebreaking tools were found, proving that but for the acute senses of " Bruce," the Manor House would have been burgled that night.

JUNO: A LABRADOR

As the name implies, this large black or yellow species of Retriever came originally from the bleak and desolate peninsula of Labrador. He has undergone considerable modifications since then, when he was a coarse animal, ill-balanced and lacking in symmetry. In spite of these drawbacks dog fanciers were quick to recognise his alert movements and the wide-awake features characteristic of nearly all dogs from northern latitudes, features that form a striking contrast with the drowsy and degraded mongrels with expressionless eyes that we meet in southern climes. Judicious crossing paved the way to the graceful dog we know to-day.

The Labrador has long been a favourite with gamekeepers, but it is only in the last few years that he has, in any numbers, joined the ranks of Police dogs. It was only recently that one of H.M. Inspectors of Constabulary reported that this breed had been found the one most suitable for patrolling. It remains to be seen whether the Labrador will oust the others, notably the Airedale, employed on this duty.

" Juno " ame to the kennels many years ago. She was a pure black Labrador and probably the first of her breed ever to be employed as a Police dog. She was trained chiefly for water work, which includes assisting drowning people. Her sense of smell was very keen, so tracking formed part of the curriculum. She was quiet and gentle, and for this reason she was not used as a protector for the man on the beat, though many animals of mild and even timid disposition will attack as bravely as their fiercer brethren should anyone or anything they cherish be imperilled.

As is the case with most of her sex training was not attended with any particular difficulty. Moreover it was facilitated by her love of swimming. In addition to her amiable nature " Juno " had a quality that calls for mention—perseverance. We know it is common to the breed, but this dog possessed it in greater measure than most and where others would lose interest she would pursue her search indefinitely, as the following story clearly shows.

A pedlar calling at a farmhouse had stolen a watch from the kitchen dresser. A dog was put on his trail but owing to the obstacles encountered at length lost interest and had to be called off. " Juno " took his place and despite unfavourable atmospheric conditions, misleading spoors and changing terrain, she persisted in her quest. Although the dog lives in a world of smells tracking is most fatiguing work but whatever weariness " Juno " may have felt she persevered in seeking out the true line. At one time it would be only inch by inch, at another the pace quickened for some distance, then a halt and a renewed casting around until at last she ran her quarry to earth. The thief was arrested at a wayside inn some two miles from the scene of his crime.

It has been said that water work was " Juno's " speciality. This she turned to good account. On one occasion she pulled out of the water a child in imminent danger of drowning, on another she helped a man to reach the bank who would otherwise probably have lost his life.

Thus far " Juno " at work; now let us turn to her at play, for recreation is an important factor in a Police dog's training. One day " Juno " was scampering gaily by the river side when she suddenly came upon a wild duck sitting quietly by the brink of the water. Before one could say a word both the duck and " Juno" were in the water. They dived together, but in a few moments " Juno " rose to the surface with the bird in her mouth. She came to dry land carrying it most delicately and went up to her trainer, delivering it into his hands without even the feathers being injured. " Juno " had never been used for sporting purposes and her act was doubtless an instinct derived from ancestors trained to retrieve prey for their masters in far-away Labrador.

" Juno" loved to play with an india-rubber ball and when she lost it was miserable until she found it or another was brought to her. The trainer would carry several balls, old and new, in his pocket, into which " Juno " was accustomed to nose, but an old one, gnawed, bitten and broken, was the favourite, and she would take no notice of the rest.

So " Juno " at work and at play—always the same gentle, lovable creature. Undaunted and unwearied whatever the difficulties, she deserves a high place in the hierarchy of Police dogs.

Printed in Great Britain
by Amazon

38692475R00040